SOCIAL MEDIA
FOR BUSINESS

SOCIAL MEDIA FOR BUSINESS

FOOLPROOF TIPS TO HELP YOU PROMOTE YOUR BUSINESS OR YOUR BRAND

LINDA COLES

Best-selling author and LinkedIn Influencer

First published in 2018 by John Wiley & Sons Australia, Ltd
42 McDougall St, Milton Qld 4064

Office also in Melbourne

Typeset in 11.3/14pt ITC Berkeley Oldstyle Std

First edition published under the title *Learn Marketing with Social Media in 7 Days* in 2011

Second edition published under the title *Marketing with Social Media: 10 Easy Steps to Success for Business* in 2015

© Blue Banana 20 Ltd 2018

The moral rights of the author have been asserted

National Library of Australia Cataloguing-in-Publication data:

Creator:	Coles, Linda, author
Title:	Social Media for Business: Foolproof Tips to Help You Promote Your Business or Your Brand / Linda Coles
ISBN:	9780730345770 (pbk.)
	9780730345787 (ebook)
Notes:	Includes index.
Subjects:	Social media.
	Internet marketing.
	Business networks.

Cover design: Kathy Davis/Wiley

Cover image: Blue Button chat (Evgeniya Mukhitova/Shutterstock); Social Network Icons (Taner Sumer/Alamy Stock Vector/Alamy Stock Photo); Google Plus Icon (Yulia Ryabokon/Alamy Stock Vector/Alamy Stock Photo)

10 9 8 7 6 5 4 3 2 1

Disclaimer

The material in this publication is of the nature of general comment only, and does not represent professional advice. It is not intended to provide specific guidance for particular circumstances and it should not be relied on as the basis for any decision to take action or not take action on any matter which it covers. Readers should obtain professional advice where appropriate, before making any such decision. To the maximum extent permitted by law, the author and publisher disclaim all responsibility and liability to any person, arising directly or indirectly from any person taking or not taking action based on the information in this publication.

Sometimes it's the fear of failure that stops you doing something you really want to do; the self-doubt rears its ugly head and you stall before you've even started. I wasn't sure if I could ever write a book, but now I'm working on my ninth and it's all down to the belief of one man — my hubby, Paul. I hope this book spurs *you* on to conquer what might seem like a minefield of digital overload, but really isn't when you understand just a little bit more.

To your success!

Contents

Foreword

Marketing is a 'state of mind' that must exist in any organisation—public service or private sector—if that organisation is to identify and serve the needs of its various stakeholder groups, in any truly meaningful or effective way.

It is a common paradigm that marketing is a commercial tool designed simply to sell as many products or services as possible. One not uncommon definition is that 'marketing is the art of arresting the human intelligence for long enough to extract money from it'. It's not that. That's mugging.

Period.

As I've often talked about, a business or organisation—public, private, profit or not-for-profit—is a 'marketing organism' that requires a marketing state of mind in everything that it does to meet its customers' needs.

Period.

And that means that marketing is about so much more than advertising or promotion. It's about understanding the needs and wants of existing and potential customers, and then making meaningful connections and developing relationships with each of those groups, time after time after time.

Marketing is the entire business of *doing* business looked at from the stakeholders' point of view (*all* stakeholders, including staff, customers, shareholders, suppliers, communities, etc.). In this environment, marketers should bring a dynamic, powerful and effective approach to the development and implementation of marketing and/or communication strategies.

So how do we do this? Once upon a time it was by advertising, PR and promotions. Today, the digital and online world has generated social media. Social media is not a new 'what' in marketing; it's a new 'how'. The core concept of marketing has not changed and will never change. Social media simply created a new environment in which relationships can be established and effective marketing communications can take place. Most of these social media platforms even have their own built-in data analytics tools, which enables companies to track the progress, success, and engagement of ad campaigns.

Social media is now at the core of effective marketing. Most marketing activity is a costly waste of money but if social media is fully understood and effectively implemented, it works.

There are an increasing number of social media channels and it is vital that marketers understand each one of them, how they are structured, who their participants are, what they are used for and how to penetrate those markets without seriously rattling their cages — a real risk with social media.

One of the best and most impressive social media brains that I know is marketer and author Linda Coles. And she has written this book in a powerful and effective way that will help all marketers understand the concept and the practice of social media. Highly valuable.

She also brings humour, warmth and a big brain to the book which increases its value enormously.

The single biggest thing that social media has brought to the world of marketing and marketing communications is people.

We now recognise and understand more than ever that people do business with people. Companies are no more than legal entities.

And in this environment, Linda is a star, connecting and communicating with people in a constantly impressive manner.

Read the book. Carefully consider what Linda has to say. Integrate it into your business's activities. Do those things and your business will become even more successful than it already has been.

Brian H. Meredith

CEO of The Marketing Bureau, New Zealand

Former Director of Saatch & Saatchi, UK, and Acting Chief Executive of the company's $50 million Manchester Agency

About the author

Hello! I'm Linda Coles, an international speaker and author.

I run a small company called Blue Banana and mainly work from my home office in New Zealand. Paul is the love of my life, Stella and Monkey are my two cats, and Daisy and Britney are my goats. In my spare time I write thrillers and I run—a writer needs to keep moving.

My background is mainly in retail management working for some of the UK's biggest retailers, but life in the slower lane beckoned and so Paul and I moved to pastures green south of Auckland. The slower life never really happened, and I continue to work with some really great brands, helping them to build relationships with their customers online.

I speak a great deal and write about building relationships—an important part of being successful in business. I wrote the books *Learn Marketing with Social Media in 7 Days* in 2011, *Start with Hello* in 2013 and *Marketing with Social Media* in 2015. I also write regularly as a LinkedIn Influencer, along with Richard Branson, Barack Obama and Arianna Huffington—which sounds very grand—and I am very honoured to have been asked.

I hated English lessons at school, and never became interested in writing until about eight years ago, when I started blogging and working with social media. I wrote my first book to share my knowledge with thousands of others in order to make it simpler for them to understand. Had I known at my very first job at age 13, delivering milk early on weekend mornings, that I would become a writer, I would have paid more attention at school. Now, I write content for others, so they can pretend they are writing to their client bases, when really it's me.

The team at Wiley is affectionately known in my house as 'Team Wiley': people who are simply a pleasure to work with and who stretch my mind like an elastic band—sometimes to popping point! The whole editing process is my favourite part: our final chance to make the book as good as it possibly can be...otherwise there is no point in writing it.

Connect with me on:

▶ Twitter: bluebanana20

▶ Facebook: bluebanana20

▶ LinkedIn: bluebanana20

▶ Instagram: bluebanana20

▶ Pinterest: lindacoles

▶ YouTube: bluebanana20

▶ Website: bluebanana20.com

▶ Podcast: iTunes Blue Banana

Acknowledgements

Writing a book is great fun and hard work so I would like to give thanks to all of those people who contributed their stories and opinions to this book.

I am continually inspired by the writings of other LinkedIn Influencers who give informative content as well as make people think about how they can do a great job with the tools at hand. Once you realise how simple something is, the fear goes—and I know that if you are feeling as if social media is another language, you will be pleasantly surprised. Enjoy.

Introduction

Social media might have some scary connotations for you, but it really need not be like that. If you act online as you do in the flesh, and don't try to be something you are not, it's really very easy and you'll find success!

Who should read this book?

Using social media in business is something that all brands, both big and small, should be adding into their marketing mix to make sure they are communicating in the same places where their prospects and customers hang out. You may think that social media does not concern you, but you are wrong. If your customers expect you to use certain sites and you don't have a presence there, they may just look elsewhere—namely at your competition.

In this book, we will be working through Facebook, LinkedIn, Twitter, YouTube, Snapchat, Google+, Pinterest and Instagram, as well as looking at email marketing, podcasting and making your website work.

One of the most common questions I am asked is, 'How long is this going to take me?' My answer to that is simple: when you have your pages all up and running, you have a plan and you have read this book, you need to spend about 30 minutes per day when you first start out. That's just 30 minutes per day on marketing your business and communicating with your prospects and clients.

What will I learn?

By the end of the book not only will you have a greater understanding of Facebook, LinkedIn, Twitter, YouTube and the other social media platforms, but you will know more about getting your website to work for you, how to behave online and how to promote your efforts. You will also have created a simple social media plan and a content plan to keep you on track. You will find heaps of easy-to-understand how-to's in this book, as well as stories about how other companies, both large and small, are using social media and getting results.

Once you have read the book and completed the activities, you will be well on your way to creating your very own successful social media presence.

Enjoy the read! Then make it happen.

Opening story

On a very wet and rainy Friday morning in June—one of those torrential downpour types of days—the traffic on the motorway was at a standstill: we were going nowhere. I had been on the motorway for nearly two hours on what should have been a 60-minute journey, and it was obvious I was going to be late for my appointment.

I made a call to my first appointment and postponed it for another day, then got off the motorway. As I now had a little time to spare before my next appointment, I grabbed a coffee and picked up *Business Today* magazine from the bookshop. On the front cover was then–country manager for Microsoft New Zealand, Kevin Ackhurst, and I knew I had to act. I had had an idea a couple of weeks previously, but had not done anything about it; now, there he was looking at me from the magazine rack. It was an omen, surely.

I wondered if he was on LinkedIn so I could contact him that way.

Of course he was—most businesspeople are. And to my delight, I discovered he was in one of the groups I was in, which meant I could send him a message directly without knowing his email address. I wrote a quick note to him with my idea, and sent it off.

To my surprise, he responded within a couple of hours to say he liked my idea and was passing my details on to the team and they would be in touch.

True to their word, they did get in touch to organise a meeting. Woohoo! I'm talking to Microsoft!

Do you think if I had simply picked up the telephone, fought my way past the gatekeeper, introduced myself and hopefully managed to explain my idea to such a senior person, I would have gotten that far?

I don't think so.

By using LinkedIn to my advantage, I cleared any obstacles right out of the way and went straight to the person I needed. I made it easy for him to find out more about me simply by clicking on my name, and from there he was able to decide if I was worth seeing or not.

This is a simple use of a great business-networking site that has the ability to connect businesspeople with other businesspeople all across the world.

CHAPTER 1
Social media—policy, plan and profitability

Key areas we will cover in chapter 1:

✓ using social media, and why it's important

✓ explaining social influence

✓ growing your business with social media

✓ networking and making connections

✓ making effective social media and content plans

✓ monitoring your social media profitability.

If you think social media is for the young ones and that you are too old to even contemplate it—never mind finding the time or having the resources to do it—then you should read on.

Do I need social media?

I have heard people say, 'I have no time for social media', to which I respond, 'You have no time for marketing your business and building relationships with prospects and customers?'

Think about that for a moment.

Yes it takes effort, but so does every aspect of running a successful business, and there are tools available to help you pull it all together. When we put your plan together later in this chapter, you will see how easy it is.

You may also think that your customers and prospects are not on social media, and so social media can't help your business. Did you know that the fastest-growing demographic on Facebook is females over 55, or that LinkedIn's most popular sector is 'service', with personal profiles for everyone from cheese-makers to the president of the United States? There is a group of people, however large or small, on these channels—or accounts—just waiting for you to put yourself or your brand on their radar.

How cool would it be to get your customers' feedback in real time, as it is happening? You'll get both good and not-so-good comments, but the not-so-good comments are as valuable to your business as the good. If the comments show you have an issue in your business that needs fixing, it's better that you know about it, isn't it? You can then apologise, react to the issue and make it good for everyone to see.

Sharing your life and finding new friends online is now the norm. But while I don't want to share my private life with the masses, I am okay about sharing my business life with anyone who is willing to listen. It's a great way to let interested people know your business exists.

Digital marketing and social influence

By using the online channels, more and more people will get to know that your business or brand exists. Do a great job at getting people talking and sharing, and you'll find others will happily follow their lead, also known as their social influence.

What is social influence?

The Wikipedia definition of social influence is quite simply:

> Social influence occurs when a person's emotions, opinions, or behaviours are affected by others. Social influence takes many forms and can be seen in conformity, socialization, peer pressure, obedience, leadership, persuasion, sales and marketing.

If you've ever read Jonah Berger's book *Invisible Influence* you will know that, like his book *Contagious*, it's absolutely chock-full of real stories and light-bulb moments — and it is one of the few business books I didn't want to put down. It takes you down the path of 'invisible influence', something I hadn't thought too much about — until I read the book. Now I am fully aware of those things that do influence me in one way or another. There are plenty of ways you can influence your prospects to buy from you, such as clever marketing campaigns, effective branding, an attractive sales team or a well-known customer-service philosophy. But what about the things you can't control within your business — the things that influence but are not obviously seen?

Let me explain using some of Berger's examples and some of my own.

▶ You take your team out to a restaurant for lunch to celebrate a milestone. You have your eye on the apple pie for dessert but when the waitress collects the dessert orders and you realise you are the only one ordering, you don't want to eat alone so you immediately change your mind and go without. It was your co-workers who influenced you to change your mind — without you realising it.

▶ It's autumn, and the weather is up and down. You never know what to wear. You don't want to be too hot, or too cold. So you look out the window to see what others are wearing and make your decision from there. In this case, complete strangers are influencing you on what to wear.

▶ It's well known that you never eat at a restaurant that has no customers in it. You are influenced to move on because you figure the food mustn't be any good if no-one is eating there.

▶ You go to the gym on a particular day purely because your friend is going.

▶ You buy a book because of the cover design or the description of what's inside.

▶ You buy a new cereal when you can see what it looks like through the cellophane window in the box.

▶ You keep away from a person because they are unkempt.

▶ You don't like to open a bottle of wine if there's no-one to join you.

When did you last buy a book or book accommodation online without checking the review stars? Did the negative reviews stop you from your purchase or was it the five-star reviews that actually made you purchase?

All the time, people and things are influencing even the smallest decisions we make; our job now is to make them positive influences.

Some ways you can influence, starting today:

▶ Having great team photos on your website instead of stuffy corporate ones might influence visitors to contact you because you look more 'human'.

▶ Being seen doing something great for a customer could influence their return, or even influence others to buy from you.

A smartly presented team and environment is much more appealing to a customer than an unkempt one; they will want to stay around longer.

What outside influences are having an impact on your business? It could be something out of your control, such as the weather, or it could be something you can control. Work out what those unseen influences are and see if you can make them work positively for you.

How can influence help you online with digital marketing?

The five-star review system has been around for many decades — it is said that a movie reviewer started it with three stars back in 1928. Three stars meant 'excellent', two meant 'good' and one star meant 'mediocre'. No stars at all meant the picture was no good. Restaurants use it, as do hotels. Who wants to stay or eat in a one- or two-star establishment? So the system has been around a long time, and we recognise it as a reasonably safe bet.

Take a post you see in your newsfeed on any given channel. You scan the image and it grabs your attention, or maybe the headline or description appeals to you. You decide to take a closer look and there at the bottom is the 'social proof' that something is worth your moment of time. The ad has 1000 likes and 500 shares, as well as 657 comments. Instantly, you realise something must be good about this post and you allow yourself to click on it for more information just to see what all the fuss is about.

Take that same post with no likes, comments or shares and you'd probably pass it by — you probably wouldn't click on the link because your time is too precious.

It was the social proof of all the activity from others on the post that influenced you to check it out — nothing to do with the post's design and content at all, but the influence of others.

When you create a post on social media that garners plenty of social interaction or proof, you need to make the most of it. These are the posts you need to promote, put some money behind and allow to run, gathering more and more social proof — social momentum, if you like — as they go. If it's an ad that's running well with social proof, keep it running by editing the content rather than stopping it and creating a new one, as social proof can't be carried over from one ad to another. (More on ads later.)

Social proof is extremely valuable, as we've learned, so gather it as you go and keep it working hard for you. Other people's views on

5

something are far more powerful than you spouting about how good your own product or service is because, frankly, why should anyone believe you? But they will believe a bunch of strangers.

Nothing going on here—move along!

The same can be said about when a visitor finds your Facebook page. Ask yourself what they would find if they visited it right now (if you have one)? Your last post was a month ago? You only have 17 'likes'? Your banner image promo is no longer relevant? No-one is conversing with you or anyone else on the page? If that's what they would see, they would move on, probably quickly, and probably to your competitor. Your lack of activity and digital housekeeping would undoubtedly influence any visitor to move away and may even influence them from contacting you at all. If you currently have such a scenario, either tidy it up or unpublish it until you can.

Social proof is all around us and we can use it to our advantage. Get focused on the social sites where your customers and prospects hang out and start influencing them by interacting with them.

How are you marketing at the moment?

What do you have in your current marketing toolkit? I suspect it contains things such as newsletters, your website, news media articles, internal communications, surveys, TV and radio, events, referrals and possibly the telephone business directory. Most if not all of these tools will have a price tag attached to them, with some being out of a lot of companies' reach. Not every company can afford to advertise on TV, and certainly not often enough for their ad to be effective over time. Not only can these tools be cost-prohibitive, they can also be a little out of date.

Now consider the social media and online sites that are becoming more and more commonplace. You might not even class some of them as social media, but they are online communication channels nonetheless. The beauty of social media from a cost point of view is that how much you spend is up to you and your budget. Spend up large and you'll reap the rewards, but you can also do amazing things with a very small budget. So if you are still hanging on to your business directory ad as the most secure way of generating new enquiries, it could be time to think again and move on to something new.

Table 1.1 lists some of the current and new marketing tools.

Table 1.1: current and alternative marketing tools

Current marketing tools	Alternative marketing tools
Newsletters	LinkedIn, Facebook
News media	Twitter, LinkedIn, Facebook
Website	Facebook
TV and radio	YouTube, podcasts
Business directory	Blog, LinkedIn
Referrals	Webinars, LinkedIn
Surveys	Forums

From a branding point of view, social media platforms enable you to engage with your customers in real time and find out what they want, think or feel at any given time, which makes them a great tool for any company to utilise.

Benefits of using social media

There are many benefits to using social media:

- It works with any budget.

- You have a huge potential audience.

- It's another communication tool to be utilised alongside more traditional methods.

- You can engage easily with your customers.

- You have a visible presence on the web.

- You receive real-time feedback.

Spoilt for choice

There is a plethora of choice when it comes to social media sites. The obvious ones are Facebook, LinkedIn, Instagram, Twitter, Pinterest and YouTube, along with Snapchat and Google+. To these we can add online activity such as blogging, webinars, Skype and podcasts. Oh, and don't forget email marketing!

Long gone are the days of picking up a pen and writing a letter to someone, putting a stamp on the envelope and walking to the postbox to send it—this really doesn't happen much anymore. Email is now the normal form of business communication, with the telephone a close second. As more and more people are in email overload, I can see that changing—though not for some time yet. And email marketing still very much works because the message is delivered directly to the inbox so the reader doesn't have to go out in search of it.

As each generation comes into the workplace, it seems to find another way to communicate—Snapchat is that medium for many today. The way we communicate has changed, and it will change again in the future. Who knows what platform will be popular in two, five or 10 years' time?

How will social media grow your business?

Some companies have been able to grow their business massively by using social media in a clever way. But how can you do it? Simple. You need to:

▶ engage your customers

▶ deliver great content

▶ listen to your customers

▶ build your business network

▶ find your cheerleaders and raving fans

▶ do it all over and over again.

Engage your customers

You may be wondering just what I mean by this, but it is simple. Get your customers interested in what you have to offer. What problem do *they* need fixing? What need do *they* want to fulfil? What desires do *they* have that are not being met?

Deliver great content

Engage them by delivering the right content. This is your chance to provide them with a solution—one that's just for them. It's not about telling them how wonderful your product or service is.

Listen to your customers

By talking and listening to your customers and prospects, you will get a feel for what it is they really want from your product or service. Now, you're not likely to sit and call each and every one of your customers, but by using the social media sites where they hang out, you have an easy set of tools at your disposal to be able to listen effectively.

Build your business network

Building your business network of connections will give you tentacles in all sorts of different industries and places: you may never know how and when you will use them, but they are there for you. By building a large connection base, you can call on select people to point you in the right direction, or reach out to them for help with a quirky need. A connection once reached out for help with an unusual position he had, and I passed his request on to one of my connections, and...guess what? It was a fit. Some of the stories you will read in this book were sought from my network on LinkedIn. It doesn't always work out, but I know that without a great connection base, I wouldn't have the same resources to make use of from time to time.

Find your cheerleaders and raving fans

You will have customers and clients who absolutely love what you do and who couldn't be happier with your product or service. So how are you currently leveraging from them and rewarding them? Do you even know who they are?

If someone has been a cheerleader of yours without you realising it until now, do something special for them. Send them your new product to try; give them a little extra service if you can. Make them cheer some more, and maybe they will shout about you and your brand more than they already do wherever they hang out online.

Do it all over and over again

Here's a real example of how a small operator can create a buzz about their brand and engage customers both online and offline.

Real story: Buy ice-cream in Giapo dollars

Giapo is an ice-cream parlour in Auckland. Set up in January 2008 at a time when business was definitely getting tougher, Gianpaolo Grazioli took the plunge and it seems he hasn't looked back. Not only is the shop set up in a very funky and modern way, but Gianpaolo has also made a huge splash and gained large numbers of followers and fans through his social media sites such as Twitter, Facebook, Instagram, Snapchat and YouTube. There is always something going on in his shop—whether it be karaoke, ice-cream tasting or even organised runs around the CBD. Messages are relayed back and forth through the online social media space for massive exposure. You can even shoot a quick video while still in his store and upload it to YouTube for your mates to see. Talk about getting others to promote your brand for you and become cheerleaders! He also encourages customers to bring in fruit from their gardens that hasn't been sprayed with any nasty chemicals, and he will pay you in 'Giapo dollars' (ice-cream)!

Your details are not safe online ... or are they?

The more nervous ones among us are concerned that all of our details are out there for anyone to steal. But your details will be secure on the vast majority of social media sites, and are controlled by you (although you do need to double-check your settings occasionally as sites make updates). Remember, too, that your business details — your mobile phone number, landline number and email address — are likely already available for all to see on your website because you want it to be easy for a prospective client or customer to get in touch with you. Of course, I wouldn't suggest you post your address if you work from home, or other sensitive information, but my point is *the choice is yours* as to how much to share, and you want your business details out there, so it's a bit of a non-issue.

What if it goes wrong?

Social media sites enable you to receive real-time feedback, both positive and negative. For example, the NYPD came under fire when it decided to engage with the local community via Twitter. It set up and promoted the hashtag '#myNYPD' to encourage people to share great photos they might have of themselves with the police in the community. Instead, some people decided to use it to post pictures the police would rather the public didn't see, such as individuals being dragged by their feet as they were removed from protests.

As long as you act quickly when things don't go according to plan, you can minimise any damage. The internet tends to jump into overdrive from one topic to another quite quickly, so whatever may have gone horribly wrong for you is likely to be old news very soon. (More on security in chapter 14.)

Let's start networking and making connections

By using sites such as LinkedIn, you can network effectively and make use of other people's connections that you may want to do business with.

I once asked a question in a group on LinkedIn and a lady from Canada responded. She said she could help me, but knew someone a bit closer to home to me—could she pass my details on? I agreed, and a couple of days later I received a phone call from Sarah. She said my name was familiar to her and asked if I was attending a women's networking luncheon later that day, which I was. You can imagine, then, that when we both arrived at the function, we made a beeline for each other. It was almost like seeing an old friend again because we had been joined together by the lady in Canada, and we had this great story to tell others. Sarah later became a client and a good friend, and in fact lives only 40 minutes away from me.

So don't be put off if you think networking online is only for talking to people from other countries and is of no use to you. The world is an incredibly small place now with the use of technology, and even doing business across the other side of the world may not be that hard.

Networking in your pyjamas

If I said to you that there was a networking event taking place nearby and some of the greatest businesspeople you would like to know will be attending, would you make the effort to get to the event? Of course you would. This sort of networking is going on all the time on social networking sites such as LinkedIn. Couple that with the ease of Twitter, and you have a recipe for nurturing relationships with people you may not ordinarily come into contact with.

Not many people read the business pages or another business directory with a view to calling and meeting new business connections, so apart from regular networking events and business appointments, how else can you grow your business network? Face-to-face networking options such as your local chamber of commerce and other business networks will never die—they are undoubtedly the best way to meet other business connections—but online networking can and does run alongside these as an alternative and extra way to meet people, and it will give you the variety you may be lacking. You are not constrained by a venue or time and you can take part at any time of the day that suits you or your business.

Benefits of networking online

The benefits of networking online include the following:

- You can do it 24/7, 365 days a year, at a time to suit you or your business needs.

- It's not location-specific.

- It's a less pressured environment.

- You can make use of small gaps of time by surfing newsfeeds and connecting.

- You can do it in your pyjamas.

Creating a listening post

What about listening? Social media can also be used as a simple listening post that enables you to hear what is being said about a multitude of things, such as your brand, your own name or even information about your competitors. There are tools to enable this to happen easily, so you don't need to regularly search

13

through Google to hear what others may be saying about you. Listening online gives you the following benefits:

▶ You can respond to bloggers who have mentioned your brand or your name.

▶ You can promote positive mentions.

▶ You can deal with any negative mentions.

▶ You can monitor your competition.

Tools for listening include:

▶ Hootsuite—a dashboard tool that makes Twitter easier to use

▶ Google alerts—set up an alert for a given keyword to your inbox

▶ Twitter search—search Twitter for keywords; no account needed.

Of course, there are many more listening tools available. Every site has its own mechanisms for 'listening'.

Getting an effective social media plan together

If you don't spend a little time making a social media plan, you will more than likely end up attacking it from all angles and your success may be limited, which will only make you feel like the whole thing was a waste of time. If you really hate writing plans, you don't need to worry too much because your plan only needs to be a simple one-pager. You just need some clear direction so that you know where you are headed and can track your successes. As Jack Welch once said, 'A strategic plan is simply picking a general direction and implementing it like hell'. So true—my kind of guy.

How do I go about making my one-page plan?

First you need to ask yourself what you want to achieve by using social media over three, six and 12 months. It could be:

▶ a larger prospect base to talk to

▶ a certain number of connections and followers

▶ a monetary amount

▶ a reputation for being an expert in your field

▶ a certain number of visitors to your website.

Then ask yourself three questions:

▶ What is my *purpose* in using social media?

▶ What am I hoping to *achieve*?

▶ What is my desired *outcome*?

The 'purpose' aspect could be very simple, such as:

▶ You don't want your competitors gaining the edge because they are already using social media.

▶ You realise it is another way of communicating with your prospects.

▶ You want to grow your business network of connections.

The 'achieve' aspect could be:

▶ You want to attract more customers.

▶ You want to listen to what is being said.

▶ You want to gain more brand exposure.

The 'outcome' aspect could be:

▶ You have created and engaged a tribe of fans who have become cheerleaders for your business.

▶ You have a listening post set up.

▶ You have a greater network of business connections.

▶ You have achieved the figure that was your goal.

A template for making a social media plan is provided in table 1.2. See the appendix for a sample completed social media plan. Social media moves and changes so fast that it would be difficult to plan much further ahead than 12 months, but it is important that you have milestones along the way at three and six months, just to check how you are tracking against your goals and to see if you need to make any adjustments. You may find that your goals have changed slightly, so this also needs to be taken into account.

Table 1.2: social media plan

What is the purpose?	What are our 12-month social media objectives?
What will it achieve?	What are our six-month social media objectives?
What is the outcome?	What are our three-month social media objectives?
Our target market is:	Measured by?
Owner:	Team:

Activity 1

Complete your social media plan.

Create a SWOT analysis

Another element to consider adding to your plan is the good old-fashioned SWOT analysis (strengths, weaknesses, opportunities, threats), which, although it has been around a long time, is still a very effective and easy-to-use tool.

The SWOT analysis can be done as part of your plan, or as an activity on its own. Either way, it is important to see, from a social media point of view, where you and your competitors currently are.

By listing the four headings and asking the questions below of your business, you will end up with four clear areas that show where you may have problems and whether you are travelling in the right direction. Take into account what your competition is currently doing, or what you think they might do. Copy the template in table 1.3 or download it from my website: www.bluebanana20. com/resources. See the appendix for a sample completed SWOT analysis. A SWOT analysis details your business's:

▶ *Strengths*. What are you good at? List your strengths and then see how you can leverage them for even greater results.

▶ *Weaknesses*. What are you not so good at? What do you need to do to mitigate your weaknesses?

▶ *Opportunities*. What are the events and trends that are favourable to you? How can you leverage your opportunities?

▶ *Threats*. What are the events and trends that are not favourable to you? How can you mitigate your threats?

Table 1.3: SWOT analysis

Strengths	Weaknesses
Opportunities	Threats

Activity 2

Complete your SWOT analysis.

Forming the social media team

A common mistake that companies make is to presume that the best person to set up your social media sites is whoever is under less pressure than the rest of the team, and therefore has the most time available. This can very often be the receptionist. Now, although your receptionist may be fantastic at their job, they may not necessarily be a marketer or customer service manager. So who should be working on your social media sites?

I asked a couple of companies how they decided who should be on the social media team. One company said, 'The people need to be online already and understand how it all works; they need to be on brand so they live and breathe our business; and lastly they need to be on resource. The latter refers to a good knowledge about where they can find great content in our market that is useful to share out again'.

Another company said, 'We simply sent an invitation out to the whole company to see who wanted to be involved in the first place. Who are our knowledgeable team players that know and understand our business and the online space? From there, we made our selection'.

Both of these ideas are great ways to find the correct person or people for your social media plan, but if you are a very small company, it may just be you in the first instance. Don't despair that you are already trying to balance more plates in the air than you would care to admit; if you stick to your plan, you won't go far wrong and your efforts will be rewarded.

Get a media team in place

Don't feel that you have to do it all yourself, and certainly don't simply get the most junior team member to do it just because they spend so much time on Facebook. Looking after the online marketing for your brand is *quite* different from chatting with friends on Facebook. Ask your staff who would like to be involved, create a small team and call them the 'media team'. If you don't have such a team, consider who else from outside your business might want to be involved. As long as you or a designated person who knows exactly what is going on and is accountable has the final say, you should be fine.

Getting a content plan

Content, or what information you choose to share from around the web or your own work, is what will make your efforts succeed: no-one wants to read uninteresting articles. Brainstorm with your colleagues and anyone else you wish to get involved, and make a list of the useful websites that always have great content on your chosen topic. You can add those sites to your content plan template later. Those sites may not even be local to you — they may be on the other side of the world — but that doesn't matter. If you have a bridal business and your chosen resource sites are in New York, who cares? You are adding value back to your followers, fans and connections with your expertise and knowledge about what is happening on a larger scale, or, in the case of fashion, what trends are developing.

When you have found the best resource sites, subscribe to their databases and follow their page accounts so that the best and most interesting articles come straight to your inbox for you to read and action. That way you don't need to revisit their sites each day to see if there is anything new.

Keep a list of the resources you are going to be using so that regardless of who is looking after your social media, anyone in the team can update it should the need arise. It also means you don't have too much to think about each day as you know where your content is coming from.

Don't make it all link back to other people's sites; you want to balance it out with great information from your own team including photos, video clips and stories.

What is content marketing?

You may have heard the term 'content marketing' and have probably been subjected to it — hopefully, if it's been done well, without you even realising. It's a term that is now commonplace but became 'famous' only in recent years.

Back in 1895, John Deere published a magazine called *The Furrow*, which provided information to farmers on how to become more profitable. It's still around today, with readers in 40 countries. But it's not a magazine with ad after ad for tractors and machinery; it's useful content on farming and how to be more profitable. There just happen to be pictures and information on John Deere's products in the magazine, just in case the reader might be interested.

The same goes for the original *Michelin Guide*, a guide on motor maintenance, accommodation and other travel topics. The more people travelled, the more their tyres would wear out and need replacing, and hopefully they'd think of Michelin tyres.

That's content marketing: adding value to someone's world and making your product or service secondary in the message, but keeping your brand on their radar for just when they need it. Everyone in your company should have the opportunity to contribute, so don't miss the opportunity by not asking—you may have a budding writer among your team. There are many ways you can create your own content; for example:

▶ articles for your news or blog page on your website

▶ images of your product or business

▶ videos

▶ audio such as podcasts.

You don't need to be a designer or a wordsmith to create your own great content; you just have to have ideas that will interest people. A good place to start when writing is to answer frequently asked questions about your product or service in the form of a short article. Chances are, if it's a common question, others will find the answer useful too. You can then present that information in various ways: picture, video or audio.

What is it not?

Content marketing is *not* banner ads, direct sales messages or telling your audience how good you are with buy, buy, buy! They will be saying bye, bye, bye if you post this type of content on your online pages.

Set up content themes

Now that you know what content marketing actually is, setting themes will keep it easy for you. Depending on what your business is, you might want to theme your content to match your overall marketing plan. This is easy if you are, for example, a florist or gift shop: make a list of all the Hallmark events that happen throughout the year—in other words, events that you buy a card for such as Father's day, Easter and so on—then theme your content accordingly.

On Valentine's Day, the florist could have not only matching flowers, but also short articles on the history of St Valentine's, as well as images. A great discussion topic for LinkedIn could be, 'What are you doing for your partner this Valentine's?'—a question designed to get others networking and nothing else.

For a health professional, it may be 'spine awareness week', so focus your theme on that. Ask questions on LinkedIn about posture and how people deal with back pain: do they use a Swiss ball or a special chair?

If you are a mechanic, you might want to talk about the importance of good brakes during the winter months on your Facebook page and Twitter.

There are other areas on the content plan, such as:

▶ off-topic questions

▶ useful videos

▶ article ideas.

As you read through this book, you'll see these areas are covered in various sections, so fill these in as you go. You can copy the template content plan in table 1.4 or download it from my website: www.bluebanana20.com/resources. See the appendix for a sample completed content plan.

Table 1.4: content plan

What is your target market's BIGGEST problem, need or desire?	Themes for the quarter
Articles to write	Useful videos
Off-message questions	Useful websites

Quick ideas for your content

These are just a few ideas to get you thinking in the right direction; they are covered in more detail in individual chapters of this book.

Facebook

News topics could include:

▶ how-to's

▶ what has been happening in your industry

▶ product launches

▶ behind the scenes

▶ team announcements

▶ funny stories

▶ your company blog.

You could also upload videos of your products or services, and some photos.

LinkedIn

LinkedIn is a business networking site, so your content should mirror this:

▶ Use some of those great links you found as a discussion point in the groups you are a member of.

▶ Write articles for your own website on a weekly or monthly basis and refer to those.

Twitter

The conversation here is a mixture of formal and informal:

▶ Tweet your own articles and blog posts.

▶ Tweet content from the LinkedIn groups if those groups allow it.

▶ Pass on or retweet other people's interesting articles.

YouTube

Upload videos that:

▶ showcase your product

▶ introduce your team

▶ show your TV commercial behind the scenes

▶ show new product creation

▶ answer some how-to's.

What makes people share?

There is a science behind what makes people share and, as social media success really does rely on people sharing your content, it's important to create the right type of content. There is a great book on the subject called *Contagious: Why Things Catch On* by Jonah Berger, which is also published by Wiley. Berger is a Wharton professor and it's a fabulous read that will totally blow your mind regarding what the vital ingredients are for writing content that people will want to share. Jonah has given me permission to briefly write about those secret ingredients here, but I still suggest you add his book to your reading list. Consider the following, and decide which elements you think would make the most sense to your audience and how you can create something worth sharing.

Social currency

People love to share things that make them look good. They like to look smart, funny and in the know. That might be by using gamification (making something game-like) or by being the first to have seen a video or to answer a question. It's that feeling of a little smugness, I suppose, and we are probably all guilty of it at some time.

Triggers

We talk about things that are top of mind or topical, so using a reminder that keeps an idea about your brand in people's heads really works. What is it that makes people think about your product or idea? Are you a pizza restaurant and Saturday night reminds people that it's pizza night? Or how about when you have your morning coffee you think about having a KitKat? Saturday and coffee are both triggers in these cases.

Emotion

When we care, we share. Think of all the YouTube videos or images you have shared in the past and look at what it was that made you share them. No doubt there will have been an emotion involved—maybe something made you laugh heartily, feel angry or sad or feel totally in awe. Whatever it was, it altered your pulse rate, which in turn made you inevitably pass it on. What can fire people up about your product or service?

Public

Built to show, built to grow. Can others see when someone has consumed your product? For example, if you have an iPhone or iPad and you send emails from them, there will be a default message at the bottom of each one saying 'sent from my iPhone/ iPad'. This is public advertising and sharing without you even thinking about it, as well as a little bit of showing off that you own a smartphone or device. Each time you send an email, you are doing the advertising for Apple products. How can someone else do the same for you?

Practical value

News you can use. If you come across something really useful or helpful, you will more than likely share it with your friends. It might be advice on unruly teenagers, money-saving tips, healthy-eating recipes or how to make the perfect exploding volcano model. Whatever it is, useful gets shared. What problem does your product or service solve for others? That is what you need to focus your message on—and then find a medium to deliver it.

Stories

Stories are easy to remember and pass on. If you can dress your message up in a true story rather than a bunch of facts and figures, it will become more memorable. The trick here is also to find a way to incorporate your brand and make people remember it. Think of great series of ads such as the Oxo stockcube lady and her family—those 42 ads ran for 16 years and the family became a part of many British households.

The Countdown grocery chain ran similar ads with a fictitious family called the Colemans. This also ran for many years, keeping the Countdown brand in many homes, both on TV and online. What Trojan horse ideas could you use to get your product known?

Rules of engagement

It is important to set some guidelines for your writing team as to what can and can't be said on the various sites, and it is up to you how detailed you want the guidelines to be. They can be simple and include the following:

▶ Never swear.

▶ Never bring the company into disrepute.

▶ Never badmouth the competition or another person.

▶ Never argue with another company.

▶ Deal with all complaints as if the complainants were standing in front of you.

▶ Don't shout in capital letters.

There are plenty of social media policy examples available online and some for purchase, so take a look at what others have done and decide what you feel is appropriate for your business. While you want to make sure everything is covered, you don't want to go over the top and gag your team.

Activity 3

Create your content plan.

Monitoring your social media profitability

We have looked at why we are using social media, who we want to talk to and what we want to achieve. We have a list of where the content is going to come from and who is going to manage it. The last thing to work out is how we are going to measure our return on investment (ROI).

There has been a lot of discussion about measuring the ROI of a company's efforts because people realise it is in fact quite difficult to measure, but there are a few tools to help you.

A great free piece of software is Google Analytics. Your social media efforts are going to drive lots of traffic back to your website, so make sure you have monitoring tools installed to capture that information. By monitoring your traffic, you can see which sites are in fact referring traffic back to your website and chart them. Go to www.analytics.google.com and follow the easy steps. You will then be given a short piece of HTML code to put into your website. You may need your web person to do this bit for you, but it only takes a couple of minutes so it shouldn't cost much, if anything.

Facebook Insights is another free tool available to you and accessed from your Facebook page. This will give you information on the mix of your fans and how active they are, which you can then use for marketing purposes. For instance, if the majority of your fans are female and aged 35 to 44, and you decide to try Facebook ads, you can target those people for a more focused ad.

LinkedIn is a little easier and more obvious because you know if you connected with someone on LinkedIn and they are a client. That is hard evidence. It is worth mentioning at this point that not everyone will become a client straight away, and some never will, but from a networking point of view, who knows where that connection might take you? A client last year admitted to taking six years to finally contact me to work with them because the time was now right. When you send a valuable newsletter-style message to all of your connections, watch what happens to your own inbox with positive comments coming back in to you. Remember that radar?

By registering for a bitly account at www.bitly.com you can monitor just how often a tweeted link has been opened—how many sets of eyeballs have now had exposure to your information—and therefore how useful or relevant the tweet you shared has been for your audience. You can also shorten URLs there and it's free. (More on Twitter in chapter 4.)

Other areas that contribute to the ROI

Defining the ROI of social media is a bit like defining the ROI of your telephone—it's not easy. But there are more questions you can ask that will contribute to your ROI:

▶ What have we learned from our customers that we didn't know before?

▶ Did we manage to talk to more prospects and expose our brand even more?

▶ Did our clients find out anything new about us?

▶ Are our staff more engaged now?

▶ What shall we do for all of our cheerleaders?

▶ Would we now do without it? (No!)

How great would it be if you found out on your Facebook page that the new cheese-flavoured crackers you have just spent a fortune developing were in fact a little over-salted for most people's taste, and you were wondering why repeat sales were not happening as much as you would like? What a goldmine of information you could have at your fingertips.

Why not reward your cheerleaders and get them to cheer about your product or service even more? Send them some free product for even more promotion.

What you don't see

During a conversation with a company director, he told me about a prospect who had called him after doing his due diligence on the director's company. If the prospect was going to part with a large amount of money, he wanted to see if the company practised what it preached. He looked at the team's LinkedIn profiles to see if they were all of the same standard and displayed the same company message, checked that the company Facebook page followed suit and looked at some of the company's other sites to see if everything was 'on message'. It wasn't. There wasn't consistency all the way through.

Now if the prospect had not picked up the phone and called the director to tell him what he'd found, he might have simply decided not to become a client and no-one would be any the wiser. What it did do was make the director's company sit up and take note that it needed to get its message consistent, and pronto. How many other prospects had it lost that it didn't know about because its social media message was not consistent?

People are checking out your brand all over the internet, so if you have anything to tidy up, do it today.

Conclusion of chapter 1

Now you understand a little more about what social media is and how it can help your business. The most important thing to do next is create your social media plan, because without it your efforts could be seriously diluted and your success is at risk. We will refer back to your plan as we work through the book, so before you move on to the next chapter, do spend some time, perhaps with your team, and get at least the bones of it together. As this plan is a working document, keep it handy for the relevant people to work with and update.

CHAPTER 2
Facebook

Key areas we will cover in chapter 2:

✓ choosing the right page type for your needs

✓ setting up your Facebook business page

✓ coming up with content ideas for a successful page

✓ managing your 'likes'

✓ looking at what Facebook ads should include.

Facebook was originally set up for people who wanted to keep in touch while at college and university, but the site has morphed into something much more than that. With nearly two billion active monthly users and about 70 per cent of those users living outside the United States, it truly is global and not to be ignored.

Quick facts on Facebook

Here are some interesting Facebook facts:

▶ There are nearly two billion users worldwide.

▶ Fifty per cent of active users log on daily.

▶ The average user has 130 friends on Facebook.

▶ It has 300 million photo uploads daily.

▶ The average time spent on Facebook is 20 minutes.

Using Facebook for marketing

As marketers see the growth and possibilities of this site, more and more brands are setting up business pages and seeing real results from interacting with their customers. By getting real-time feedback, both good and bad, from their business pages, marketers can now really interact and engage with their customers, and for relatively little cost too.

Note

Even though the correct terminology is now 'likes', most people still refer to 'likes' as 'fans'.

So where do you start? There are many page types to choose from. Which one is for you?

Profile page

The profile, or personal, page is for individuals who want to keep in touch with their friends on a social level, and not for business. You will occasionally see people using it as a business page, but there are a few things to note about doing so:

▶ It is against Facebook's terms and conditions, so you risk being closed down.

▶ You have to be a member of Facebook to join in.

▶ You have to become a friend of that person to join in the conversation.

▶ Profile pages are not easily seen by Google, depending on the individual's security settings.

Group page

A group page is an option if you are running a club, a cause or even a local interest. The group can be public for anyone to join, closed so it's invitation-only, or completely secret, such as for a small company's intranet system. This is quite a common choice for towns and local communities to meet and chat to other locals.

Points to consider about a group:

▶ You can add resources to the page such as PDFs for members to download.

▶ Like-minded people can discuss things in relative privacy.

▶ You need to be a member of Facebook to join.

▶ Group pages are not easily seen by Google, depending on whether the group is public or closed.

Business page

The most practical option for most businesses, the business page is easily created and you don't need to be a member of Facebook to see it.

Other points about business pages:

▶ Pages are easily seen by Google.

▶ A small business could use a Facebook page as its first web presence.

▶ Facebook is free to join and use.

▶ Nearly two billion people on Facebook could potentially see your page.

▶ Updates feed into your fans' own newsfeeds as you post something.

▶ When your fans like or comment on a post, their friends see your page name in their newsfeed too, so the viral effect gets to work.

A business page is by far the best option for most businesses, so let's look at how you can set one up.

Setting up your business page

Once you have decided to create a Facebook page for your business, you need to know how to build it.

There are two ways of setting up your own business page on Facebook. The first is the most common way, but you need to have a personal account with Facebook in order to create your business page. To build your page, simply click the 'create page' link from the drop-down menu of your profile page and then follow the easy instructions.

The second way is to go straight to www.facebook.com/pages/create and again follow the simple instructions.

There are pros and cons to everything, and choosing which way to build your page is no exception. There are a few main differences between the two options:

▶ If you run your business page off a personal profile, you can access it from your usual login if you want to update it.

▶ You can and should allocate trusted members of your team as 'admins', which means they will also have access to the business page for updating it. They will not, however, be able to see your profile page — only their own — which means they must have their own Facebook account.

▶ Any admin can delete another admin, so choose your team carefully.

▶ By running your business page off your profile page, you have the ability to share any of the content with your own

Facebook friends, and the other admins can also share content with their friends, so it can get your page off to a good start.

▶ If you run a business-only account — that is, not one off your own profile account — you have no friends to share information with.

Quick tip

It's the norm and quite safe to run your business page off your profile page as no-one can see into your private posts. It also saves you remembering yet another login as you simply use your own. All admins appointed use their own logins too.

Once you have decided which way you are going to go, choose which category of page you would like to make. The categories are as follows:

▶ *Local business.* This is really for a bricks-and-mortar store, café, restaurant, and so on, as the page gives you an area to add your opening hours and bus route. With a 'places' page, people can check in from their smartphones when they physically visit your premises, alerting their friends to where they are. Great for restaurants and cafés.

▶ *Company, organisation or institution.* This is probably the most common as it covers most businesses not needing an actual location to promote. The same for brands and products.

▶ *Artist, band or public figure.* Depending on which sub-category you pick, there are different areas within the info tab. For example, if you pick 'politician', there is plenty of room to fill out set questions such as which party you are running for, further detailed information about yourself and all of your contact details.

Whichever category you choose, you can switch it later if you need to, perhaps if you see something that is more relevant.

When you have chosen your page and filled in the basic details, take care with the page name as it can only be changed if you have fewer than 100 fans/likes. After that, you have to apply to Facebook and ask them to change it, which they may or may not do!

Activity 1

Set up your page and upload a branded header image and logo.

Your page name has now been created but your page is pretty bare and useless until it has been branded up and has some content added.

Take a look at some examples of what big brands such as Coca-Cola and Red Bull are doing. While they have bigger budgets than most of us, there is no harm in looking at their ideas and adapting them to fit your business.

Do you need multiple pages?

Some companies have several brands under the main company umbrella so you may decide to have more than one Facebook page to separate things, depending on the topics.

If you are a catering company that specialises in weddings and corporate events, you might want two separate pages. Even though you are one brand, there are two distinct sides to the business, one being bridal catering and the other a more corporate focus for business lunches and events.

The bridal page could include not only bridal catering, but other things bridal such as possible venues and photography. This makes the Facebook page almost like a portal site, where a bride or groom could find out all sorts of information to help create their big day, all in one place.

Other articles and blog posts you could share on your wedding catering page include:

▶ events from the weekend, including photos

▶ prestigious events you have catered for — name-dropping always helps

▶ wedding photos

▶ wedding cakes

▶ a video of an event

▶ edible gift ideas for your guests

▶ a timeline of making the great wedding cake — what was involved

▶ food at recent celebrity weddings — what they ate

▶ dealing with dietary requirements for the bridal party

▶ links to the bride and groom's blog about the day, if they have one.

In all cases, be sure to add just enough detail about what is happening in each posting. It is no good putting up your lovely pictures of the buffet lunch if you have not gone into loving detail about what was on the buffet. Keep the readers' mouths watering as they read all about the mini pastries oozing with soft, dill-flavoured cream cheese and delicate pieces of gently smoked salmon ... you get the picture. You are trying to convince readers to think of you when it comes time for them to place their own order. You can also think of more personal content, such as what the team has been up to recently, trade competitions you may have been involved in, new team members or even funny stories about what happened during an event. The list is endless.

So what can you do with the corporate catering page? You could add:

▶ venue ideas for your party

▶ ideas about wines to accompany the food

▶ recipes to make at home

▶ reminders to book catering for key dates such as Easter, Valentine's Day and Christmas

▶ food trivia questions and competitions

▶ recommendations from happy customers

▶ links to articles published about the company

▶ new corporate vehicles on the road

▶ food-tasting events

▶ daily dinner recipes.

And on the list goes … food is such an easy one!

Back to your content plan

Your content plan is crucial to your page's success, so spend the time to make it and actually use it.

You don't need to create everything that you post on your wall: you simply don't have the time to keep that up. Find resources on the web that are in line with your brand and that complement each other rather than compete against you. Think about the following:

▶ Which websites do you read regularly to keep abreast of your industry?

▶ Which sites are there that perhaps do compete in your space, but are overseas and so not a local threat?

▶ Which other sites are local to you that you could help promote on your page and build a relationship with for referrals?

▶ Which sites complement your page (for example, wedding planners and wedding caterers)?

Your content plan will pretty much make or break the success of your page. By not having a plan, you will find it very hard to keep being creative and get the right sort of content for your fans, meaning they may lose interest and go elsewhere.

By brainstorming with your team, you will not only get buy-in from them to ensure your page's success, but many heads are better than one when it comes to thinking up ideas.

It is also a good idea for more than one person to update the page, so that sickness and holidays are covered and the page keeps up its momentum. If there is more than one person updating the page, perhaps sign off your post with your first name so your fans know who they are talking to when they comment, and you know who posted what from the company point of view.

Following are some content ideas for various industries.

▶ *Real estate.* Listing all of the properties that you currently have for sale is somewhat boring for your page visitor — they can see that information on the company website in most cases, so there's no need to duplicate it. Interest as many people in your page as you can so that when it comes their time to sell, your informative page is still on their radar. All they need to do then is get in touch. When people are looking to purchase a house, they may need extra information, such as:

   – what to look for in the sale contract

   – where to find a good lawyer to handle the transaction

   – where to find a good, reliable builder if there's some work needing to be done

   – garden design

   – interior decorating

- bargain properties

- local surroundings — schools, amenities.

▶ *Garage mechanic.* You may wonder what you could possibly put on a mechanic's page to appeal to a greater audience. One possibility would be to target it to females who want to keep their vehicles running smoothly themselves: you will probably have a captive audience if you get your message right. There are not many garages that are focused on helping women specifically. But if you are not a petrolhead, why would you become a fan of a garage page? How about if it had information on:

- how to change a tyre

- what warning signs to look out for, such as green brake fluid leaking

- car reviews

- open days

- learning the trade

- what different parts of the engine do

- wet-weather car care.

▶ *Accountant.* This is another subject that could be brought to life to cover its many different aspects, if done well. Consider information on:

- how to calculate how much money you should be putting away for your tax at the end of the year

- keeping your business plan current

- helping with cash flow

- seminars (invite your fans and clients)

- deciphering technical terms to make them easily understood

- planning for selling your business

- general business advice.

▶ *Retail shop.* Your shop probably has a website, which will pretty much be an online brochure with opening times and contact details, and you may also have a shopping cart to allow you to sell online. So your Facebook page could be a great meeting place for discussion, depending on what you sell. Imagine you own a cycle shop, and your customers love hanging out in your shop to see what is new and discuss their last race and their upcoming events. They can now do it both in your shop and online. Cycling is a lifestyle choice and many riders are very passionate about it, so this gives you the chance to capitalise on that passion even more. With a hobby such as cycling, you tend to have friends who are also heavily into cycling, so your fan page has the opportunity to really make use of the viral effect. Your page could include:

- upcoming events

- cycle maintenance

- race reports

- special offers

- new product discussions

  coaching tips

- flash new cycle images

- race videos.

▶ *Vineyard.* Now this would be an interesting page for quite a few people. Include:

- how the grapes are grown

- a video of wine being made

- what makes a good wine

- discussions on what makes a great flavour

- special offers and open days

- corporate tours

- wine reviews.

For all of these examples you should also add interesting company news, photos of products or team members and video footage of products in action, or being made if you manufacture something. The more interesting (and sometimes basic) the information, the better: you might know your industry or products well, but your average visitor may not, so use the opportunity to educate at the same time.

Other things to add to your Facebook page could include links to articles on other websites that you think may be of interest, although the danger in doing this is that your visitors may not come back to your page, so they might not see the rest of what you have to offer. On the other hand, they may come back more frequently because you have a balanced offering of other people's work on the same or a similar topic that is as interesting as your own. Find the balance between what suits your business and what your fans want. You could even try asking them.

When you do post something to share with your audience, always add a call to action. For example, ask a question or make a statement and add on the end, 'We would love to read your comments' or 'Click "like" if you agree'. That way, people know you want them to do something, and generally they will if it takes only a second or two.

With all of that in mind, consider what resources you could marry up with to make your page an even greater source of information for your visitors.

Activity 2

Jot down content ideas you could put on your page from what you have learned so far.

Should you allow your fans to post on your page?

Why do some big brands and well-known celebrities not allow you to post on their Facebook wall?

Apart from the annoying activity of others posting spam messages and plugs for their own business or activities, I can't see a real reason—it doesn't seem a fair way of interacting with the fans, and it really defeats the point of the page.

In the name of research while writing this book, I wanted to become a fan of a well-known car manufacturer's page and ask what made the car so special to them, but it wouldn't let me post. I would have thought that car enthusiasts all over the world would want to be able to interact with their favourite brand. Move over to Starbucks, and its page is full of interaction and postings from anybody and everybody about their experiences with Starbucks products from all corners of the world.

I can understand why Beyoncé's page, with well over 65 million fans, has the facility turned off. Can you imagine the mass of postings from real fans and those that just want to take a pop? Managing the comments alone would be a full-time job, with some of the postings from her team running into the tens of thousands of comments as replies. That really is simply not doable.

If your page is purely another online brochure, and you have one because you are expected to have one, you probably want to take the road with the least amount of hassle or work, in which case you would turn the facility off. I would not advocate even having a Facebook page if you are not really going to use it, so think about your reason for doing it before you get started. The same goes for those who are worried about getting complaints on their page. It's an opportunity to learn from your customers too, so if you are getting complaints about anything, sort out the issue quickly.

If, on the other hand, you really are trying to generate massive brand awareness, network and engage with your customers and build up a loyal tribe of fans and followers, you will need to have the resources to back it up. If, like Beyoncé, you have the 'problem' of millions of fans, simply let your fans know what to expect in the way of answers. Manage people's expectations by posting a note in the information tab or other visible place on your page that you will be able to reply to only a handful of comments each day. That way, everyone knows where they stand.

A couple of extra things to note about your page:

▶ Determine how much access to your page you want your fans to have. Did you know you can choose whether to allow them to be able to post images and videos to your wall?

▶ Don't overstuff your wall with constant messages all day. One or two posts per day should be enough.

▶ Do post great images of your product or service with a link to further information.

▶ Don't post pictures of the team when they are drunk at their Christmas party.

Comments

Reply to all comments by using the person's name, just as you would if they were standing in front of you or on the telephone, and be friendly and helpful at all times. If you do happen to get any negative comments, don't simply delete them unless they are particularly abusive or racial. By deleting negative comments and keeping a clean page, you may be adding fuel to a smouldering fire. Others will be watching to see how you react and deal with a negative comment, so do something about it. If you find that your page is getting quite a lot of negative feedback about your product or service, you need to do something about that whole issue within your company, so it's great information to have. You might never have known there was a problem without that feedback. (We cover etiquette in more detail in chapter 9.)

Scheduling content

There is also an option to schedule your posts, which means that your posts will go live at a time and date specified by you. This is particularly handy if you have a full day ahead or perhaps you are away for a couple of days: your Facebook page will still receive fresh content that you have pre-loaded. Look for the option to schedule from the drop-down box before you hit 'Post'. You can also use a scheduling tool such as Hootsuite, which we will discuss in chapter 4 as it's primarily a Twitter tool.

Using Facebook Live

Fancy showing your audience something live? Well you can. You have the option to create a live video stream directly from your page, which means your followers can tune in and see it in the moment or watch it later as a video that is auto saved. This can be great for events or items of interest you wish to share, and you can plan to use it at a given time too, allowing you to notify your audience in advance. Jamie Oliver took 'us' around a fish market in Asia live, which was fascinating and because it's live, it tends to be more casual so it's a great way to get to know an individual if they are a brand. Kim Knight, 'The Kiwi Health Detective', streams it through her webinar software for those who are not on Facebook. Here's her take on it:

> A few months ago I started using Facebook Live. Initially I had quite a steep learning curve: firstly I discovered my ancient Android phone needed replacing, after which the difference in software speed and quality of camera was amazing! Then I had problems recording Facebook Live from my office because I don't (by health choice) have wi-fi and it's a real hassle to install software to do Facebook Live from a desktop. Which meant I had to go and sit in my car or go somewhere else to record Facebook Live!

I then discovered I could simultaneously stream Facebook Live through my webinar software, giving people the choice of watching via Facebook Live or webinar. This is handy for clients who (believe it or not, it happens) do not have a Facebook account.

This year I started a regular weekly Facebook Live webinar, partly because I love sharing this information 'live' and also as a lead magnet, and it's working great. I multipurpose the video and upload it to YouTube, my private membership portal, and iTunes. The video also gets loaded onto my website video blog (vlog), and into other sites which are using my vlogs. So that's seven birds with one stone:

▶ live webinar

▶ Facebook Live

▶ replay of Facebook Live as a video

▶ YouTube video

▶ private membership site

▶ podcast

▶ website vlog.

Since starting the weekly Facebook Live I have noticed a definite increase in post watches, shares and likes, even and especially after the live event.

Just loving this technology now it's all coming together, and interacting with others more and more.

Facebook ads

Only a few years ago, you could be sure that your fans would see within their newsfeed when they surfed Facebook whatever you posted on your page. That's changed, unfortunately, and due to the algorithm Facebook uses, it means that only some of the content you post will be seen, depending on how much they interact with your page, and some other variables. And it keeps changing, making it near impossible to keep up with. Now that Facebook has shareholders to please, they want you to use their ad platform to get your content seen by more people. Now, while you might not agree with this, since you're using the site for free, you have to play by their rules. I've found there is little point trying to buck the system—just work with it, not against it. If we want the power of Facebook, we need a budget, even just a small one of $5 per day. The topic of ads is huge, but I have given you the basics here to get you started. By trialling and practice, you'll get better with time.

Facebook ads are a great way to drive traffic to a particular place or to do something in particular. Choose from:

▶ awareness

▶ consideration

▶ conversion.

Go to the drop-down menu from your page, choose 'create advert' and you can see what each one means. If you want to drive traffic to your website, choose 'consideration/traffic'; if you want to collect email addresses for your database, choose 'consideration/lead generation'; if you want to get more fans, particularly in the beginning, choose 'consideration/engagement' and if you want to drive foot traffic to your location, choose 'awareness/local awareness'. These do tend to change a little, but the end result you're looking for will be there.

The beauty of using the ads is that you can drill down as far as you want, to find just who you want to talk to. You can choose who to target by:

▶ *location*: which country or within a set distance of a town

▶ *demographics*: male, female, age group

▶ *interests*: reading, cycling, cooking, movies and so on

▶ *connections on Facebook*: users who are connected to friends of a page, for example.

Once you have decided to have a go with Facebook ads, you need to consider four things:

1. What is the goal of the ad?

2. Who are you trying to reach—what is your target market?

3. What is your daily/weekly budget?

4. Who is going to monitor the results?

What is the goal of the ad?

Now, you might think this is obvious: you just want more fans/likes, right? Well, not necessarily. It may be that you want more people to visit your website rather than your fan page, as you have a sale on or a new collection being launched. In this case your ad may be pointed straight to your chosen website landing page for visitors to find out more.

If your goal is to generate brand exposure and gain more fans to communicate with, your ad should be pointed to your Facebook page rather than your website.

The advantage of pointing your ad to your Facebook page is that when your visitor clicks 'like' and becomes a fan, you can communicate with them through their Facebook newsfeed in future by sending them an update. By sending your visitors to your website, there is generally no way for them to interact with your site and those visitors may never return, so you have lost them.

If you want more people to find your bar, for example, set your ad to show in their newsfeed in the evening when they are most likely to be looking for a bar to drink at.

Who are you trying to reach?

Again you may think it's obvious who your target market is but, bearing in mind how you can drill down into the Facebook database, you may have a different message for different people. Check out what you concluded in your social media plan for your target market to make sure you are targeting your ads correctly.

Let's say you are a coffee shop and you want to create an ad to drive traffic to your Facebook page to generate more fans. Your customers could be split into three categories depending on age and wants, and so the three different messages could read as follows:

▶ *Parents* — bring your little ones in for a milkshake and get a free chocolate bar when you mention Facebook.

▶ *Students* — take a break from studying and grab a hot steaming mug of creamy latte. Have a free chocolate bar on us when you mention Facebook.

▶ *Night owls* — we are now open until midnight, so call in for a hot chocolate before bedtime and get a free chocolate bar on us when you mention Facebook.

You get the idea? It's a different message for different age groups, but the same product. You only have a few characters for the title, and a few for the body, so you may need to fiddle around with your message to make it fit. The ad will tell you as you create it.

What is your daily/weekly budget?

You can set your budget at as much or as little as you want to spend, so if you are a small company and have a budget of only $50 per week, then start with $50. Obviously, the more you spend, the more audience your ad will reach.

The more targeted your ad is, the fewer the people who will see it, but the more relevant it will be to those who do. You can actually create an ad that is seen by everyone in your town who is aged 35 to 40 and who has a particular interest. Very cool, and very targeted.

Who is going to monitor the results?

Someone has to monitor and refine your ad or ads and make adjustments where necessary. In the early days that can take a little time to do while you are getting used to it.

Check your stats daily and watch for any trends. If you're not quite getting the results you had expected you may wish to stop the ad and start another ad that is almost the same, changing just one thing such as the image or the heading. Slight changes can make a world of difference, but only change one thing at a time or you won't know what the successful change was. That means either change the image, the text or the headline and test the results again.

Once you are really happy with the results and with how much you are spending, you can afford to let it run for a while. Keep monitoring it though, as you may find the ad's effectiveness will dwindle in time and you need to refresh the process again.

Facebook has a great self-help area on Facebook ads — click the 'help' link for more information.

To keep control on the go, download the 'Adverts' app to your smartphone.

Keep in mind that most people are on Facebook for entertainment; they are not there searching for what you have to offer, so your ad needs to stand out visually and the text within the message must be appealing in order to get people to click on it. Heavy business messages may not do as well here, so keep them a little less formal for Facebook.

Sponsored updates

Another type of ad is the sponsored update, which is simply the promotion of a post. That means a post, usually an image and text, can be placed in front of other eyeballs such as your fans' friends, or even just more of your fans, but you have to pay for it. Both sponsored updates and regular ads will be seen in the newsfeed, but only regular ads will appear down the right side of a computer screen. When they are shown in the newsfeed they are also visible when viewed on a smartphone, and as about 50 per cent of Facebook users access Facebook via their mobile, that's an important point to remember: they are still visually appealing and can be read easily.

Facebook is a business too; it is out to make money, and as it doesn't charge you to use its site, it has to make its revenue in other ways—namely, ads. As long as you target your ad to the right demographic, including age, sex, interests and location, you won't go too far wrong. So, as I said at the beginning, make sure you decide on who your target market actually is—it really is important.

Activity 3

Create an ad for your brand following the advice in this chapter.

Real social media success story: Budget Car Sales

Budget Car Sales is a secondhand car yard on the outskirts of town and they are doing extremely well generating and converting leads for used-car sales on their Facebook page. It's not always been that way, though: when I started working with them, while they had a decent fan base of about 2000, most of their fans were not even in the same country, and it was obvious the 'fan base' had been bought. Why else would 75 per cent of their 'fans' want to become a fan of a secondhand car yard on the other side of the world? It just didn't seem likely.

(continued)

Real social media success story: Budget Car Sales *(cont'd)*

The company wanted to change their Facebook page name because their brand had changed, and obviously everything needed to be consistent. The problem was, Facebook declined the name change, so they were stuck: they had to decide whether to stay as they were or start again. It was a tough decision because it's not easy to accumulate fans in the first place, and what about all the past content that would be deleted?

A new page was created and they posted a 'we are on the move' image on the old page with the URL to the new one. They decided to run two pages alongside each other for a period of one month so that they could let the real original fans know they would be shifting, and so on each post, they also included a link to the new page asking fans to join them there. This worked a treat, allowing the new page to have a good few fans straight away, leaving them thinking about how creative they needed to be to get the numbers back up.

They created a content plan, which included funny vehicle videos from YouTube, wacky car images and related ideas from Pinterest as well as actual vehicles for sale in the yard, car care tips, finance options and happy shopper selfies. Posting daily and scheduling posts for the end of the day, when they knew their fans were online the most, were also key tactics. The content proved to be a success, with a good mixture of funny stuff as well as the serious business of selling cars, and they added in a few giveaway competitions to see what would be popular. They gave away cinema tickets for two asking, 'Who would you take along with you?' in the hope fans would tag their friends. (It's against Facebook's terms and conditions to stipulate friend tagging as a way to gain more fans.) While it was popular, it wasn't as popular as giving away $100 fuel vouchers! That really made things hot up, so I guess giving away something of value that is also related to the product being sold is the key to finding a giveaway that works—and with the price of fuel, it's a no-brainer.

The yard also runs events at their premises, which would be promoted through Facebook's events function. As the event organiser they can get a rough idea of how many people from Facebook will be attending, and it's great to actually meet some of their virtual customers and say hello in person, which will also surely deepen loyalty.

They also added an email marketing campaign to their database newsletter to encourage others to become fans, and told them what they could expect from the page, including giveaways and special events.

The weekend promotions at the yard have been a resounding success with previous records smashed, and while it was not all down to Facebook, without getting the message out there to prospective customers and starting to engage with them, they wouldn't have had the same number of visitors to the yard.

Their fan base has now well overtaken what they had on their old page and their fans want to engage and refer, so they have developed a small gold mine other car yards would love to have access to! If you want to be successful on Facebook, find your target market, decide on your budget and deliver what your market wants to hear, consistently.

All this happened through hard work from the marketing co-ordinator and a little help from having a small budget for sponsored posts and ads, because you do have to be realistic in getting people to find your page and become a fan on Facebook. How else will they see you?

Conclusion of chapter 2

Facebook is becoming a marketer's dream; the site gets better and better as the months go by. When you have your content plan in place, you really will need to spend only a few minutes in the morning posting your information, and a few minutes again in the afternoon checking to see if you have any comments that need answering—and monitoring those all-important adverts.

CHAPTER 3
LinkedIn

Key areas we will cover in chapter 3:

✓ creating personal profile content

✓ making the most of groups and Publisher

✓ networking and making connections with LinkedIn

✓ creating your own company page

✓ using InMail

✓ advertising on LinkedIn.

LinkedIn's main function is networking with people you would not ordinarily come into contact with. By connecting with other like-minded people, you can effectively build your business connection base, and have the potential to grow your business.

This chapter will work through the real basics that often get missed when people set up their LinkedIn profile, and then move on to how to actually use it to get real results. We will cover what should be in your profile, adding in rich media content, to really give a full 3D effect, and networking for success. We will also cover setting up a company page for even more online presence.

Quick facts on LinkedIn

Here are some interesting LinkedIn facts:

▶ It's the number-one business-to-business-only networking site in the world.

▶ It has nearly 500 million members worldwide.

▶ Fifty-seven per cent of all usage is on mobile devices.

▶ It is for adults only, although it is starting to allow students to join.

▶ It is open 24/7 for networking.

▶ It has a database of prospective contacts.

▶ Two new members join every second.

Your personal profile

Don't underestimate how many people will be checking you out online, and LinkedIn is definitely the easiest place to start looking. Whether you are meeting a new prospect for the first time, or have sent a connection request to someone, you can bet your bottom dollar that they will have looked you up or clicked back on your name to read your profile to find out more. Wouldn't you?

The first thing to mention is that your profile has to be your name rather than your company name because it is you people are interested in networking with, not your business. It is also against LinkedIn's terms and conditions to do otherwise.

If you take a look at your own profile page now, would you be happy with how it is representing you or your company, or could it be better? I am guessing it could be a whole lot better.

It is worth investing a little time one rainy Sunday afternoon to get it right. I would suggest putting a couple of hours aside to do it, but bear in mind it is never finished. It will always be a work in progress that you will add to as time goes on to keep it fresh and up to date.

Your professional headline or title

Most people make the assumption this should simply be their title — for example, director at your company — but that doesn't necessarily tell someone looking at your profile what it is you do. With a company name like Blue Banana, you couldn't possibly know what the company does — unless you are familiar with it — so 'Director at Blue Banana' means nothing.

The professional headline area gives you 120 characters, including spaces to work with to really create something precise, and should be filled with keywords if at all possible. It really needs to be the essence of what you do. Mine says 'Social Media Done For You. Speaker, Author and Trainer on Building Relationships Online'. Not only does it tell someone exactly what I do, it also contains vital keywords for the search robots to retrieve, and it also exposes my authority on the subject by telling everyone I am a published author.

Beware

Make sure you write the headline with your prospects in mind, and not solely for the search engines, as a professional headline stuffed with keywords could be detrimental to your own branding. Quite often you will see a person's email address or mobile telephone number in this area, which is against LinkedIn's terms and conditions — so, again, beware. You can always add those in further down on your page.

Your image

The image that you add of yourself should be a close-up head and shoulders, rather than a picture of you way off in the distance with your fishing rod — save that for your Facebook profile page.

When you do eventually meet up for a coffee with someone from LinkedIn, it helps to know what they look like: you don't want to rely on looking for the 'red rose', so to speak. Think also about the professional image your personal brand is portraying: have a photo that reflects that. Having no image or using a company logo gives me the impression the person doesn't want to be seen, and I have to wonder why. Having a great image also means you are seven times more likely to show up in search results, so give yourself a chance. It's also important that you keep it up to date—women are particularly bad about having quite an old picture on display that doesn't bear much of a resemblance now. Mine changes every two to three years.

Your website details

LinkedIn gives you three hot links: areas that when clicked go through to another site that they have been pointed to. Those three links need to be put to good use.

Often you will see a person's profile making use of only one of the links, because they have only one website. But why not use all three of your links and point them to three different pages on your website, such as your 'services' page, 'about' page and 'special offer' page? You can point them to your business Facebook page, your blog or even a club website that you are a member of. Either way, you may as well make good use of them.

The trick here is in the drop-down box. Select the option 'other'. This then creates a bit of choice. Yes, you can simply choose 'my website' or 'my blog', but by clicking 'other', another box appears for you to type in what the page you are sending visitors to is all about.

Your public profile address

The purpose of this feature is to allow you to hyperlink to your LinkedIn public profile address from your email signature or a job application. That way, the person is able to read the correct profile, which is particularly useful if there is someone with the same name as you but with a less salubrious past. To do this, simply click 'edit' next to your public profile address while in edit mode, and set it to your name. Then whenever you want to direct someone from, say, your email signature to your page, you simply have to set up a hyperlink within your email signature that they will be able to click on.

If your name has already been reserved, why don't you try adding in your middle initial or name? If, like me, you don't have a middle name, you could use your social media username (mine is bluebanana20). Sadly, even all those years ago when I started out in social media, the name Blue Banana was already taken.

Your summary

This is another really underutilised part of the profile, which surprises me as it seems like a simple thing to fill in. To do it right, though, takes a bit of thought. You have space for 2000 characters in all, so you have a reasonable area in which to write about yourself. But what should you include to get the most benefit?

To my mind it should say:

▶ who you are and what you do

▶ what makes you different from your competitors

▶ why someone should use you rather than your competitors

▶ something light-hearted and interesting about yourself such as your sailing ambition or your weekend-warrior activities.

Write this piece of your profile in the first person rather than in the third person, to make it more personal and real. When you have finished, just check down the left margin and see how many times you started a sentence or paragraph with 'I': you may find you need to change a few for another choice of word. This is picky, I know, but plenty of prospects or clients could be reading your summary and they will pick it up. Also, ask yourself if it sounds great or spammy. Have you stuffed it full of keywords for the search robots, or does it sound natural and informative?

Additional information and personal information

Write as much or as little in these two areas as you want. For 'additional information' you can add clubs and associations that you belong to, such as Rotary, Entrepreneurs and so on, and add in important achievements you have attained in your life. I rode my bicycle around Lake Taupo, which is 160 kilometres—and hard work, let me tell you—so I am proud and pleased with my achievement. I put it on my profile so that others can see I am a keen cyclist, and if I am meeting someone and their profile also mentions they are a keen cyclist, it gives us a point to connect the conversation immediately. I find it a real icebreaker.

The 'personal information' tab is visible only to those who are directly connected to you or whose email addresses are in the system after uploading your contacts but you are not necessarily connected to. I add my contact details, but it's a matter of personal preference whether you disclose your marital status or not.

Activity 1

Complete the additional information section. Include some things that interest you such as your sports and hobbies.

Other profile options

There are also other options available for adding information about yourself, including:

▶ certifications

▶ languages

▶ patents

▶ projects

▶ publications

▶ honours and awards

▶ test scores

▶ volunteering

▶ courses.

Skills

Adding skills to your profile does more than you might think. First, they are searchable, so when someone is searching through LinkedIn for what you do, you come up in the results. Second, you can endorse a connection's skill and they can do the same for you. This then populates the skills section and adds another endorsement to the count. The maximum number that will show is 99+ though your endorsements can be many more than this. It's a great visual when someone is looking at your profile and there are 99+ endorsements for your skills — it may just give you the edge over the competition. When you receive an endorsement from someone, you will be notified via LinkedIn email. Turn endorsements around by endorsing someone else — it puts you back on their radar just for a moment, which is always a good thing.

Rich media

You can also add some great visual content to your profile, which really makes your profile stand out because so many people just don't bother with it. So what can you add?

▶ *PowerPoint.* Add a PowerPoint presentation with a handful of great slides about what it is that you do. Make sure you add a final page with your contact details on it and either post this to your profile directly or, better yet, load it up to a Slideshare account (www.slideshare.net). As LinkedIn owns Slideshare, it's another free place where your content can be accessed by another bunch of viewers. You can then link your Slideshare account to your LinkedIn account, or simply post the link to it on your profile. While in edit mode, use the odd-shaped icon over on the right that looks a little like a square with a plus sign attached to it.

► *Video*. Use this same icon to link a YouTube video to your profile. You can also upload the whole file if you wish.

► *Documents*. PDFs are a great way to add terms and conditions, price lists, brochures and the like so that your connections can download them easily.

► *Links*. You can add a link to anything here, such as articles you have written on another site or news stories about your company — the list is endless.

Whatever you add to your profile via the rich media square icon, make sure it's visually appealing to allow connections to see the best you can offer.

Some LinkedIn profile dos and don'ts

Do:

- write your summary in the first person, that is, from your point of view rather than someone else's — it's just more personal

- write your profile content for human readers rather than search engines

- use the three website links to web pages of your choice

- make sure your grammar and spelling are correct

- add skills in search results as well as showcase them.

Don't:

- fill your summary with a sales pitch

- start each sentence with 'I'

- add your email address or telephone number in your professional headline

- use a full-length photo as your image — we can't see you

- use all capital letters (shouting).

> ### Activity 2
>
> Create your LinkedIn profile and get someone to critique it for you.

That covers the basics of your profile, but there are some very cool applications that you can add to really show yourself off in a good way.

Recommendations

This is another overlooked area: I don't think people realise the importance of recommendations. The average person on LinkedIn has fewer than a handful, with many people not having any at all. As a great percentage of us trust word-of-mouth advertising, or recommendations, and not many of us trust advertisements, it makes sense to have recommendations from satisfied clients and customers visible for all to see. They can also stand you in good stead when you are in the market for a new job as they can be used almost as references, and that may be the one thing that sets you apart from the other candidates.

I think a good number to aim for is 10, though there is no harm in going for more as I think the more people can endorse your work, the better it is for you. Be true with your recommendations, though. Don't ask your close friends, neighbours and half of the team at your place of work to write one: that simply looks dumb. A recommendation simply saying that you are a nice person is not really of much value.

So what should a recommendation include? You don't want it to be fluffy, so try to choose ones that are as factual and as relevant as possible. Include any or all of these suggestions:

▶ how the person knows you

▶ how they found you to work with

▶ what the working relationship was

▶ some personal traits, such as personable, expert or has integrity

▶ how their business changed as a result of your product or service.

Update your status

The 'share an update' box is here for you to post heaps of interesting things as and when they happen. For example, if you are being interviewed for a TV show tonight, have an article appearing in a well-known publication, are running an event, or just simply have some great news to share, this is the box to put it in, and it's on your home page. When you update this box, simply post a teaser sentence about what it is you are sharing and a link to it. The box will automatically populate, then just click 'share'. You can also share other files with your connections such as interesting PDFs, images and PowerPoint presentations here.

Using Publisher

You also have the option to write articles. LinkedIn's 'Publisher' allows you to write a full article and include images, links and video. The space contains basic formatting, but the finished articles look great and encourage you to write for your connections, who are your ready-made audience. Back in 2012 LinkedIn gave the longer article option to 150 worldwide 'Influencers' and I was lucky enough to be one of them. Now this option has been rolled out to everyone. From experience, I can tell you it's great to be able to use this as my main blog and have a ready-made audience to interact with. It's a great tool and I strongly recommend that you use it. Publish opinion pieces, market updates, learnings—anything you feel your business connections might find interesting.

You can get a huge amount of great content to share from LinkedIn's Pulse or newsfeed on your home page. This is where some of the best and most shared content on the web is filtered into, depending on what you have opted in to receive, as well as posts from LinkedIn's now 500 Influencers all around the world. These are thought leaders and businesspeople who write on the LinkedIn platform to share their wisdom with the rest of us about mainly business topics, which gives another dimension to the content available.

Content you may want to share:

▶ articles you have written online

▶ details about an exciting project that's about to start

▶ a job vacancy

▶ interesting business-related articles

▶ an upcoming TV interview

▶ a link to a useful YouTube video

▶ an opinion piece

▶ an upcoming event that you are running or attending.

Activity 3

Add the ideas for your update box into your content plan.

Whatever you post in this box will appear on all of your direct connections' home page activity, so they can see what is going on in your business life. Think of it as a rolling newsletter—so don't post uninteresting or spamming content—and you can also tick the Twitter box to feed that same piece of information out to Twitter at the same time.

You will notice other people's updates in your own newsfeed and under them you have some options to share:

▶ *Like*. Similar to Facebook, you can simply click on anyone's status update's 'like' button to show approval for the posting without feeling you have to leave a comment, and that puts you on their radar for a moment again.

▶ *Comment*. Feel free to leave a comment about a connection's post, as by doing so, you are again putting yourself back on that connection's radar and also publishing the article and comment into your own newsfeed. It's great when people do this with your content because it then puts your content into their own newsfeed, which really helps with the viral spread, leading to many more eyeballs taking in your post.

▶ *Share*. This gives you the ability to share the status update box content with others and, again, when they share it your content is in their newsfeed for their connections to see. You can share your connections' content back to your own box, or share with groups that you are a member of on LinkedIn. You also have the choice of sending it as a tweet either just to your LinkedIn connections on Twitter, or to everyone you are connected to on Twitter: it's a very easy way to spread exciting or useful information with others.

Adding your connections

This is the last thing you should do on your page, and only do it when you are completely happy with how your page looks. The first thing your new connections are going to do when they accept your invitation is see what you are up to. If there is nothing there, you may have missed an opportunity.

If you are using Outlook as your mail program you can export your connections. Go to 'file', 'export', 'create CSV file' and save the file; then from LinkedIn click on 'my network', 'import from other providers' and then follow the instructions to import your list. If you don't currently use Outlook, follow your system's instructions for exporting your contacts into a CSV file. Don't worry at this point that your aunt Mary is on this list: you are simply uploading the file into LinkedIn. Until you decide who to send an invitation to, LinkedIn won't do anything with it.

When it is uploaded, it will tell you who in your contact list is already on LinkedIn, and you can then choose who to invite by ticking the relevant boxes.

You can also remove connections by going to their page and clicking the option under the three dots or by finding them in your 'my network' tab and removing them from there.

Activity 4

Add your email database to see who is already on LinkedIn and connect with them.

Networking with LinkedIn

Now that you have joined LinkedIn and have a reasonable profile of yourself up for everyone to see, you have to use it. I am sure there are people out there who think that just because they now have a visible profile and a handful of connections, the phone is going to start ringing off the hook. Let me be the bad news bearer on that one: it won't be ringing just yet. You now have to market yourself through the various meeting points within LinkedIn so that others get to meet you and you them. This is largely done by networking within the LinkedIn groups, and getting in touch with your connections' connections. (In chapter 9, we look at networking etiquette in more detail: just what is the best way to reach out to someone to connect and start a conversation?) You may feel a little unsure about where to start, so let's take a look.

Networking with LinkedIn groups

If you type in keywords for the types of groups you would like to look at, a good selection should come up as there are thousands and thousands of groups worldwide. An example of this is my search for social media groups: there are nearly 11 thousand groups on that topic alone. It does, however, depend on which keywords the group originator puts in the group's profile details and title, so you may have to try a few different combinations. I like to add the country in the search terms too, which will bring results that are a little closer to home, but if you are looking to network further afield, you don't need to do this.

Once you have a list of the groups in your industry, there are a few things to point out before you decide to join:

▶ Groups are listed in member number order, so those with the most members will be listed first and they run in descending order. There is very little point in joining a group that has only a handful of people as the discussions will dry up very quickly.

▶ You can see who the group owner or admins are and view their profile.

▶ You can also see how many of your own connections are already in the group.

▶ LinkedIn will also automatically offer you a selection of group choices based on your profile for you to look at.

You'll be able to see a little bit more about what the group is about, and what the group rules are, before you join. From all of this information you should be able to decide whether or not the group is for you: if it is, click 'join'.

Once you have requested to join the group there may be a vetting process from the group owner or manager, but many groups are automatic entry. The choice is up to the owner as there may be competition or certain types of companies or industries that they don't want in their groups.

> **Activity 5**
>
> Use the 'search' function to find five relevant groups to join.

When you have been accepted, do abide by any rules that have been set. The rules tend to be the same in most groups:

▶ no promotion of yourself or your services or direct sales pitches

▶ no spamming of other group members

▶ be respectful of others.

These rules are so everyone can get the same enjoyment and great results from mixing and mingling online.

What should I discuss?

A few tips to get you started:

▶ Make it easy for anyone to contribute.

▶ Encourage a short answer—people are busy.

▶ Respond occasionally—after all, you did start the discussion.

▶ Don't be afraid to dive in and make a start.

People often tell me, 'I don't want to say the wrong thing' or 'I don't have anything worthwhile to say'. This is quite common so you are not on your own.

Even though I work with social media each and every day, I don't very often start conversations about it on LinkedIn as I see that as self-promotion. Instead, I might ask a more general business question such as, 'What is your referral process?' or 'What exciting things are happening in your business world at the moment?'

You see, it's not necessarily about talking shop all the time, but about encouraging other group members to take part and make themselves known, because just like you, they may feel a little self-conscious, but you are all there to network.

Some discussions are started with a statement such as, 'The economy is going down the toilet—here is what I think', but from practice and a bit of monitoring, I find a question will get you a better response. I suppose because you are asking a question, you are really giving a call to action: you are asking someone to answer it and, by our nature, we do like to help others out where we can.

I once asked a large group, 'What stops you from taking part in or starting a discussion?' and the answers surprised me. Many people were unsure whether they had anything to offer, while others simply wanted to watch, listen and learn. That's an important point to remember if you get a little disappointed when there are not as many comments to your discussion as you would like. Remember there are those silently listening, so you are adding value to someone's business life—you just may not see it at the time.

Another good way of getting others into the discussion is to ask something a little easier to answer and perhaps 'off topic'. For example, the question I had the best response to was, 'What famous person would you like to have a coffee with and why?' The answers were varied and sometimes surprising. I got over 40 people chatting away and mingling with each other over a very easy question. I would love to know what real business eventually came out of that 'networking event'.

Examples of questions to ask or discussions to start:

▶ What is the worst invention you can think of and why?

▶ What motivates you in business?

▶ What are the best business books you have read?

▶ What is the best thing that is happening in your industry right now?

Another thing to note in the group discussions is that when someone has taken the time to respond to your question, you should follow it up with a comment, even if it is only to say 'thanks for your input'. Remember your manners, just as you would do at a face-to-face networking event when someone has taken the trouble to chip in.

If you find that the group is not for you, you can always up and leave by going to the group settings and clicking the 'leave group' button, but a word of warning: if you leave a group, you can't message any of the group members directly anymore unless you are directly connected to them, and they can't get hold of you as easily either. What I suggest instead is simply turning off the email alerts by visiting 'settings' and 'communication', then 'email frequency'. Then uncheck the box so you don't receive any more notifications. That way, you have not left all of those wonderful people forever—you just don't hear from them regularly, and you can always turn them back on.

Creating your own group

Running your own group on LinkedIn is a great way to make new connections, and put yourself forward as a leader in your field, but running a group is a bit like running your website or Facebook page: it's easy to set up, but it needs some time and effort to keep the momentum going and the group growing. It does take a while to get group members to engage, but it is well worth the effort. Once you have a group that is actively starting discussions, and people are actively engaging with each other, that's when relationships are formed, referrals are swapped and deals get done.

Here are some key things to consider when you decide to set up your group:

▶ What is the aim of the group?

▶ Who is going to manage it?

▶ What resources will you use for content?

▶ Who is going to add discussions and news stories?

▶ Who will send consistent announcements out periodically?

▶ What are the guidelines for group participants or the group rules?

So, what can you do to help your group get up and running? LinkedIn gives you a few templates that you can customise a little, so that you can add in your own flavour about what the group is about and how you run it. The templates include:

▶ a welcome message

▶ a decline message

▶ a 'we are thinking about your application' message.

By personalising each template, you can add all sorts of promotional information and links, so take note of these points and see how you can maximise your own templates:

▶ Include links back to resources in the welcome message template and really maximise the use of the space with useful information, but not spam.

▶ When you set up your group profile, give as much information about the group as possible: what you are trying to achieve, what the purpose of the group is, and so on.

▶ Use the group rules section to set clear rules for your group.

▶ Include keywords in the group title and profile that you think people will be searching for when they are looking to join a group.

Sending a group message (announcement)

This is a real benefit to running your own group. As the group manager or owner you can send a group message to everyone in the group once a week. It really does give you another database to talk to, but don't abuse it. You don't want your group members leaving in droves because you have overdone the self-promotion.

> ### Tips for sending announcements
>
> Consider these tips before sending announcements:
>
> - Send announcements consistently but don't overdo it. You are able to send a message weekly, but monthly is probably the maximum.
>
> - Treat your announcement as a newsletter and include resources and value, not just about your company, but other articles too. Make it interesting to as many members as possible.

I received announcements from one group manager that were really nothing more than a catch-up email containing information about what they had been up to in a business sense, and their recent trips abroad. Now I haven't really got time to be reading other people's long catch-up emails, but I did read these and it made me wonder if that type of email group announcement was in fact a bright way to correspond. It was a little different, after all, so why not give it a go and see? It certainly put them back on my radar again.

With any social media tools, you have to give them a try, monitor the response and maybe tweak things a bit before trying again.

Featured posts

If you have something important to discuss and would like to keep it at the top of the group page for a while, make it 'featured'. When you have finished with the topic, un-feature it to move it back down the page and allow something else to be featured.

Growing your group

A bit like getting Facebook fans to 'like' your Facebook page, getting new members to join your group can be frustrating: it just doesn't happen quickly enough. There are a few things you can do to help it along, though:

▶ Send invitations out to others to join your group by clicking on 'invite others' while you are in your group. This gives you the ability to share the URL of your group and pass it on to others. If you decide to do this, ask your connections to invite their connections in too for a bigger mix of people.

▶ Use one of the three website links on your profile page we talked about earlier, to invite people to join your LinkedIn group.

▶ Make sure your group description and profile contain the right keywords so that when someone is searching for a group like yours, you come up.

▶ Tweet the group URL and invite others to join.

▶ Add the group link to your website asking others to join.

▶ Add the group link to your email signature.

Activity 6

Review your content plan: what can you add in to help you start and take part in discussions on LinkedIn?

Setting up your company page

Just as Facebook has created its version of a company page with its business page, so has LinkedIn, but the appeal of having a company page on LinkedIn is the professional, business-oriented community it sits in.

Normally, the profile pages that you set up on LinkedIn are for your own personal use, and it is indeed against LinkedIn's terms and conditions to set up a personal profile page as a business. But LinkedIn has seen that by capturing and promoting more business information in this community, it can make way for a whole lot more engagement and knowledge sharing.

Benefits of a company page

Some benefits of a company page include:

- It's another place to post and promote your product or service.

- Interested people can 'follow' your company and be notified when you post updates.

- It has a header image to make use of.

- You can link to it from your website and vice versa.

So how do you set it up?

Only one person from your company can set up the company page, and you will need to have an email address that matches your domain, so using your Gmail address won't work. This stops others from setting up company pages that they are not authorised to do.

To start your LinkedIn company page, simply click on 'more' and 'create company page'. From there it is self-explanatory and you just need to follow the very easy steps. You can now do the following:

▶ *Set up a showcase page for the main aspects of your business.* This is particularly useful if your brand is known for its sub-brands. For instance, Restaurant Brands could be the company's main page, but underneath that will be Starbucks,

KFC (and so on) showcase pages so interested parties can follow the elements of the company that they are particularly interested in.

▶ *Add a careers page if you have vacancies to advertise.* If you are currently looking for new employees, what better place to advertise than on a database with about 500 million people! The listed vacancy will pop up on the home page of people LinkedIn thinks may be interested and many companies have had success filling vacancies using this method. What is also great is that anyone who clicks on the advertisement can easily see a whole lot more about the company and the other employees who are in their network.

▶ *Follow any company that interests you.* Each time a company that I am following updates something, I am notified on my status update page. How cool is that for inside intelligence, particularly if I am a recruitment agent! I may need help to fill the vacancy that has just been created, or the person who has just been promoted may want to hear from me in their new role.

▶ *See how you are connected to a company.* The company overview page allows you to see how you may be connected to that company: it's a bit of inside intelligence. If you are looking to do business with that company in some way, you may have some inside connections who could possibly be helpful to you, or who may even pass an introduction message on to the person you need.

▶ *Post your blog posts onto the page.* Let your followers find out more about the company via your company blog posts. Each time you write a new post, post the link to show it on your page.

▶ *Add a disclaimer.* Even if you don't add a disclaimer, make use of this space to write something else.

▶ *Add a button to your website that says* 'Follow us on LinkedIn'. Simply copy the HTML code and you're done. You may need your web person to do this bit for you.

Anyone who views your company page also has the option to like, comment on or share a post with their own connections, and if you are the page manager for your company, you have the additional option to feature a post. This keeps the post at the top of your page, which is especially useful if you have an offer or promotion running or simply need to share an important message for some time.

Using InMail

As part of the premium account, you have the option of sending emails directly to people on LinkedIn if you don't know their email address. While you could possibly find out their email address by phoning their company, the beauty of using LinkedIn is twofold:

▶ You share the same community (LinkedIn).

▶ They can easily click back to your profile and read about you before they respond, something they are not likely to do via ordinary email.

I have used InMail with great success. But you need to keep your message limited to 100 words, making it direct and to the point. If you have a connection in common, you are 50 per cent more likely to get a response by mentioning them in your message. If you get a response back within 90 days, you get a credit InMail in return so it incentivises you to write a great email that does the trick in the first place. Withdrawn InMails, on the other hand, can't be credited back, so make sure before you hit 'send'.

Here's one company's experience of marketing online and using its network to get real results. This is Lindsey from Outbox's story.

Real story: Outbox

New Zealand has a strong networking culture within the business community but, unusually, my connections have often started in the virtual world and then progressed to connecting in person or establishing a business connection purely online.

When I started working virtually with Outbox in 2006, I was regularly snubbed for even mentioning the idea of online meetings or social media usage but as the following will show, there have been many instances where the speed of working virtually and not wasting time in travel and meetings really has paid off—not to mention the dollars saved from buying coffee!

I would not be writing this today if I had not connected with Linda on LinkedIn. Her profile resonated with me and we shared similar backgrounds working for retail giants in the UK. She started a lunchtime networking group meeting at Euro restaurant at Auckland Viaduct called 'Lunch and Learn—How I grew it!' Interested in hearing from established business professionals, and with the added attraction of excellent food, I attended these and not only learnt from the likes of Annah Stretton and Shane Bradley (GrabOne and Finda), but also got to ask questions on a one-to-one basis.

Some time later I referred her to a client where they employed her to train their staff on LinkedIn. Attending the session myself to ensure we were all working on 'the same page' I too learnt new ideas. During this, we discussed the MailChimp e-newsletter system and my services, which led to Linda requesting I train her to extend her skills. A win–win: shared referrals for both Blue Banana and Outbox with us extending our skills and gaining new customers.

Numerous other instances have occurred from engaging clients overseas through Facebook and Twitter postings. Others who regularly post my profile on Twitter as 'a featured VA' tagged my business, notably @BeMyVA, following my award of Virtual Service Provider of the Year in 2012. This is simply an extension of word-of-mouth referrals and extending the audience to an online platform.

The growth of services offered by the social platforms has led me to run Facebook competitions. Some time back I offered the chance to 'win a website'. The winner was the fabulous Julie Lassen, a top New Zealand celebrant. She has since gone on to have another three websites created by Outbox, all featuring different aspects of the wedding industry, not to mention additional services we have provided along the way.

As the social arena has grown, so our business services have adapted. An extension of these services was added to incorporate 'social media profile set up' for those enlisting Outbox to set up their MailChimp templates or create a new website. This enabled them to link to social media and benefit from the SEO advantages. Again, another extension of the business that had I not been using social media platforms would not have occurred. In a constantly changing world, there is always a need to adapt and move forward.

Benefits extend beyond the business and I have been able to offer more volunteer work online as well. Through connections online, where my company can be clearly seen, I have been asked to admin Facebook, Neighbourly community and networking groups—a way of giving back and in turn helping others use social media for good as well as turning 'virtual' relationships into 'live' relationships, which I feel reverses the traditional method of meeting work colleagues and clients on its head!

In summary, I now have clients in the United States, Australia, the United Kingdom, Bali and Singapore in addition to New Zealand. Without the reach of social media I do not believe this would have occurred so easily. Dip your toe in the online waters and you won't regret it!

Lindsey Carroll, Outbox.co.nz

Advertising on LinkedIn

Most social media platforms now have an advertising opportunity to get your content in front of the right people. LinkedIn is no different. While you will definitely need a bigger budget than for, say, Facebook, if your target market is on LinkedIn, it could be money well spent.

You can create an ad that appears in a person's newsfeed, or smaller ads that pop up around the site, or promote a post from your company page. You can even send ads directly into other members' inboxes through sponsored InMail campaigns.

As with other sites, you can target pretty well by:

▶ location

▶ company name

▶ company industry

▶ company size

▶ job title

▶ job function

▶ job seniority

▶ member schools

▶ field of study

▶ degree

▶ member skills

▶ member groups

▶ member gender

▶ member age

▶ years of experience.

That means you can create an ad that you only want shown to people in Sydney who work at a particular company, are female and are 30 years old. Or many other variables. Very, very powerful. Like the other sites, payment works on an auction basis, so how much others are prepared to pay to have their ad delivered to the same type of audience determines how much you pay per click. Or per 1000 impressions. In my recent experience, I have been spending between $5 and $14 per click, so while you may think it's expensive, a new client from it could be worth far more. As with all online advertising, your headline, the image you choose and the text all have a bearing on whether someone clicks on your ad or not, so try different versions and test as you go.

To start using LinkedIn's ad platform, find 'tools' and 'advertise'.

Activity 7

Set up your LinkedIn company page and post something useful.

Conclusion of chapter 3

We have covered quite a lot about LinkedIn in this chapter, so by now you should have an idea of how you will use it effectively for your own business. Your LinkedIn profile is not set in stone, so plan to revisit it in a month to see if you can improve it any more.

In order for you to get some traction with LinkedIn, try to allocate 10 minutes per day to networking online within your chosen groups and posting status updates.

CHAPTER 4
Twitter

Key areas we will cover in chapter 4:

✓ setting up your Twitter account

✓ following and being followed

✓ tweeting

✓ listening out for your brand

✓ using Twitter tools

✓ setting up your listening post.

People ask me all the time, 'Tell me about Twitter. I don't see how it's even of interest to people—who wants to know what I had for breakfast?' On the surface, you can be forgiven for thinking that, but it can really be a very powerful tool for networking, researching, publishing, icebreaking and listening, so it has many uses. You just need to understand how it works and how to use some of the many tools that are available to you. In this chapter we will look at some of these tools and share some stories about how other companies and individuals have found success with Twitter.

Quick facts on Twitter

Here are some interesting Twitter facts:

- ▶ It's a quick and easy way to microblog.
- ▶ Five hundred million tweets are sent every day.
- ▶ It has over 300 million monthly active users.
- ▶ You can tweet on the run.
- ▶ It's a great icebreaker for networking.
- ▶ You can get breaking news as it happens.
- ▶ Eighty per cent of monthly active users access Twitter by a mobile device.

What is Twitter?

Twitter was born in 2006 and is based in San Francisco. Tweets can be instantly translated from English to many other languages, so people all over the world can use Twitter easily—all you need is an internet connection and a device such as a computer or smartphone. Twitter asks the question, 'What's happening?' and was originally intended for college kids to keep in touch in a similar way to Facebook, but using only 140 characters—short and snappy. Others quickly saw the benefits of using this simple system to chat with people around the world, and the phenomenon grew, with many millions of people actively 'tweeting' every day.

Businesses then saw the advantages of using such a platform to shout about their products and services. As time progressed and more and more people started tweeting, it became apparent that it could also be used as a listening tool. Individuals saw Twitter as a way to gripe about products or services from large and small brands, a no-holds-barred, out-in-the-open-air conversation. Businesses quickly realised that they needed to do something to keep any bad press about themselves under control and quickly sort out any issues as they came to light. Likewise, businesses wanted to jump in and listen to all of the positive things that people were saying about their brand and thank them for being cheerleaders. There is also the conversation that is neither positive nor negative, where someone is simply asking a question, such as, 'Who has the better deal, Vodafone or Telstra?' Now if you are either of those companies, you are naturally going to want to engage with that possible customer and convert them to your brand if they are in the market, so Twitter can be used for intelligence too.

Setting up your account

The process is very straightforward: go to www.twitter.com and register, but give some thought to your username. There are some very odd usernames out there and some are very obviously 'get rich quick' schemes or multilevel marketing programs, so don't turn people off with a dumb name. Use either your own name or a version of it if someone else has already taken it, or something associated with your company if it is to be a company account. That might simply be the company name, but as you don't have too many characters to play with, you may need to abbreviate it. Some companies have different accounts for different parts of their business, such as @vodafone_AU and @vodafoneAU_help. They are both part of the same company but have a different voice for the different business aspects they cover. The same goes for Hilton Hotels: they have @HiltonHotels and @HiltonHelp, making for a quick response from a designated Twitter account.

Home page

This is where you can see how many followers you have, how many you are following yourself, how many tweets you have sent, any tweets you have saved to your favourites, and a whole bunch of other information. It is also where you will see tweets coming in from others you are following so that you can respond if you want to. You now also have the option of following people that Twitter has suggested: it will suggest people to follow who are similar to the person's profile you are viewing. I must admit, most of the suggested 'who to follow' people have been of interest to me, so I find it's a good tool on Twitter's part.

'Trends' is something to keep an eye on also as it shows the hot conversation threads that are going on right now. When someone famous dies, or there has been a terrorist attack, or other big news stories break, the information is soon out on the Twitter waves for everyone to see and follow. Look for the hashtags within trends and follow the story, or contribute your own with the same tag. In case you're wondering what a hashtag is, it's simply a few letters with the # sign in front of them and it allows anyone to click the tag and follow what others are saying about a given topic, whether you follow each other or not. If you click the tag because of a common interest, such as #cycling, it's also a great way to find others with the same interests and connect. Anyone can create a tag and although Twitter pretty much invented hashtags, you'll see them across many social sites now.

Profile page

From your profile page you can customise the look and feel of your Twitter page, and add your photo and a bit about yourself. There is also space to put a link back to your website or use it to drive traffic back to your Facebook business page.

If you are an individual setting up your own account, remember your own personal brand is just as important as if you were representing Coca-Cola, so take care. I suggest you have a slightly more relaxed bio than on, say, your LinkedIn page, but still keep it professional. Mine currently includes my day job but also 'writer, runner and sometimes cyclist', and I have a link to my website.

This captures the professional headline that is on all of my branding, with a little extra about my pastimes, which is important when it comes to networking. People do read these profiles, so be sure that what you write is what you are happy to be seen as. I saw one once that read reasonably professionally but then had 'dirty salsa dancer' at the end. That turned my interest off.

So, should you use your company logo or your own picture? Well, people do like to know who they are actually talking to and a logo can come across as a bit too corporate so you have a couple of choices.

▶ Use your own photo with the company-name account.

▶ Use the logo but be sure to make your name known on the profile page so people can talk to you properly. I hate it when I view a profile of someone and there is only the company name but no mention of who the person behind it is. How can you communicate with an anonymous person? It gives me an impression of an impersonal company from the start.

When it comes to filling in your location, it's a good idea to put the city as well as the country so that when someone is searching for a business in your city, you come up in the search results.

Activity 1

Create your profile for Twitter. Keep it professional with a relaxed feel.

Finding followers and who to follow

Now that you have built your Twitter page and added some information to it by way of a photo and a short bio, you are ready to find some interesting people to follow and get some followers back. By the general rule of reciprocity, many people you follow will follow you back. Start off by seeing who you know from your address book in the 'find friends' link, which you can find on your home page just under 'who to follow'. That will bring up a search box so you can simply type in either their Twitter username, if you know it, or their full name. If they are listed on Twitter, it should pop up for you and you just need to make your choice and click on the 'follow' button. You can also export and upload your contacts from Gmail and Outlook and then connect.

What Twitter itself doesn't give you is a real way to search a directory for new people to follow. But you can click on 'who to follow' and browse by interests or find friends, and a list will be created for you; then just choose who to follow. For example, if you like writing and want to follow other writers, put 'writing' in the search box and see who pops up. If you want even more of a directory to choose from—say categories—take a look at www.twellow.com, which is almost a Twitter directory as it covers just about everyone you could possibly want to follow. You should register your own details with the site (normally just your Twitter username and password) and then fill out a few details about who and where you are so that others can find you. Then get searching.

Search for businesses in your area, your prospects, clients and people of interest to you and add them in. As I said earlier, most people will automatically follow you back—unless you look like a possible spam account.

Activity 2

Search for and follow your first 50 people. Some of them will follow you back. If you search and follow more than 50 in one hit, you may be flagged as a spam robot.

Spam and abuse

You will notice your Twitter followers drop off by quite a chunk occasionally as Twitter culls the spam accounts out, so don't be too concerned if you see yours take a nosedive one day. Twitter is pretty good at keeping the rubbish down. It is probably worth mentioning at this stage that it is not wise to become a spam account yourself, as your life on Twitter will be short. By spam account, I mean setting up your account to target people with the sole purpose of pushing your product or service continually. You may find your account deactivated.

Here are a few activities that may draw some attention to you and should be avoided:

▶ aggressive following in large numbers

▶ creating large numbers of accounts

▶ sending large numbers of @replies

▶ having a very small number of followers compared with the number you are following

▶ attempting to buy followers

▶ using pornography anywhere.

These are just a few; a full list of the dos and don'ts can be found on Twitter under 'help'.

Get tweeting

The next step is to decide what you want to get out of Twitter and work on a plan to get you there. Whatever you are trying to achieve, there are some basic principles that remain the same:

▶ *Add value—don't sell.* Nobody likes to be sold to, so gain people's trust and respect by sending out interesting article links about your field of expertise. Don't send these out from your own website every time; vary them from other respectable sites too. I suggest two in 10 should be from your own business sites.

▶ *Retweet (RT).* Retweeting or sharing items that you have found interesting that someone else has posted says two things: that you found the tweet interesting (which the originator will be pleased to hear) and that it is likely to be interesting to your followers. Retweeting is the ultimate compliment on Twitter and great exposure for the originator. Can you imagine if someone in your network RT'd your tweet and on it went? Where would your post end up? That is the exponential effect of Twitter.

▶ *Engage.* Let's say you would like to meet the CEO of a particular company but at this stage he doesn't even know you exist. Apart from calling him on the phone or calling in at his place of work, how else are you going to get in touch with him? See if he is on Twitter with the search function, add him to a list so that you don't miss his tweets, and when you see a tweet from him that you can engage with, say something (more on lists later in this chapter). Now it doesn't need to be earth shattering or thought provoking, just the start of building up a rapport. If he has just tweeted that he is walking his Doberman to the park to watch his young son play in a soccer tournament, you might ask about his dog as you have a Doberman too, or wish the boy good luck, saying it was your son's tournament last weekend. The CEO will more than likely reply with thanks at the very least, and now he knows you exist. Don't then blow it by jumping in feet first! Court him with chitchat and interesting articles about his industry. It might take a little time so don't rush into it and ruin what you've started. When the time is right, suggest a meeting or coffee and you will feel like you already know a little about each other. It makes the call a warm one rather than a cold one.

▶ *Grow.* You need to actively grow your followers so that you can create a tribe of people who see you as an expert in your field, and add value to their world. When you do then publish something from your own business, more people will have the opportunity to see it, which is more exposure for you. Think back to the exponential effect of Twitter and where your post could possibly end up.

▶ *Listen.* Use Twitter to listen to what people are saying about you or your brand.

Activity 3

Send a tweet and find something of interest that you can retweet.

Communicating on Twitter

There are two ways to communicate on Twitter: @replies and direct messages (DM). @replies are directed to a particular person or account and they view their messages via their notifications tab—these are public to anyone searching. Direct messages are private, with only the two parties being able to see the message content, just like email.

Back to @replies: if you want everyone to be able to see it rather than just the person you are replying to, put some text before the @ sign, even if it's just a symbol. For example, 'Have a lovely weekend @richardbranson' will mean that Richard will see it and so will all your other followers. A reply of just '@richardbranson have a lovely weekend' will only be seen by him (or probably more likely his social media team). If you get an @reply yourself, don't forget to reply to it. It's no different from a text or email: it's someone communicating with you so it warrants a response.

If you are using an application such as Hootsuite to sort your tweets rather than Twitter itself, you will see direct messages in one column and mentions (@replies) in another when you set it up, so you shouldn't miss any. Direct messages will also filter through into your ordinary email inbox as a duplicate unless you turn them off in your Twitter settings.

Twitter terms

You'll need to know the following terms to communicate on Twitter:

- @replies are messages to you but visible to anyone doing a search.

- DMs (direct messages) are messages to you that only you can see.

- RT (retweets) are tweets that have been passed on because they were seen as interesting.

- hashtags allow you to follow a conversation about a particular topic. For example #election2017, or #tsunami or #cycling. Simply click on the hashtag to follow the whole conversation.

Lists

Lists are a great way to file the people you are following so that you can keep track of important tweets coming in without them getting lost in the flow of things. When you start getting into the thousands of followers, it is impossible to see and respond to them all. You can create lists for anything you want to filter out, such as clients, prospects, competition, motivational, educational and so on. This means that once you have added someone to a list you created, their tweets will filter through to that list for you to see easily and respond to if you wish. I find this particularly helpful for monitoring business prospects and my current clients. Think of a list as a filing cabinet or folder.

A word of warning

When you create your lists, Twitter's default is to make the list public, which means that anyone, whether they are following you or not, can click on your list of clients and see who they are. The thing to do with lists you'd rather people didn't see is to change the default to private.

There is no reason why you need to keep all your lists private, but just be cautious with any sensitive lists that you have created, such as your client list.

Advanced and auto following tools

As your account grows, it can become a little tedious clicking on each automated message from Twitter telling you that you have a new follower and deciding whether or not to follow them and action the message, so there are tools that will do this automatically for you. That way, you can still see the emails sent to you by Twitter alerting you to new followers, but you don't need to actually do anything with them. Incidentally, you can turn these email alerts off in your Twitter settings too, if you wish, but I like to be nosey and monitor them. The tool for automating your followers is www.socialoomph.com, and you can do a whole heap of other things there too to automate Twitter. There is even the option to send an auto response message to someone when they follow you. I used to use it, but I think it looks a little like spam, and it comes across as auto-generated no matter how you write the reply, which, of, course it is. Your choice — the option is there.

Advanced search

Go to www.twitter.com/search-advanced, and you can look for a whole bunch of variables, such as location, conversations between certain people and dates of conversations past. This is particularly handy if you are, say, a catering company and you are looking for people planning events who are in need of caterers in a certain city. There are many things you could search for and this is a great and easy-to-use tool to add to your toolbox. Give it a go and see what you can find out that is useful to your business.

Making posting easy

There are many applications that run with Twitter, and they make it so simple to keep tabs on things all on one screen. There are many others that do a similar job, but www.hootsuite.com, www.buffer.com and www.tweetdeck.com are my favourites. So what makes them special? You can:

▶ view all of your incoming tweets in one column

▶ see your @replies on the same page

▶ see your direct messages on the same page

▶ update your personal or business Facebook page from here

▶ update your LinkedIn status update, company page and groups from here

▶ add several accounts you may be managing, all on one screen

▶ set up search result columns so you don't miss tweets about certain topics or people

▶ schedule posts to be delivered at a later date.

Depending on which one you opt for, you can allow multiple users to update multiple channels all at the same time, which is useful for time management as well as security. The sites have a free or paid version and each has its own cool extras, so look at them all before you decide. Personally, I use Hootsuite—I like its simplicity and it runs many accounts at the same time for me in one place. It's also one of the few that works with Instagram, though it's not quite seamless yet. The main thing I use Hootsuite for is to schedule my posts to be delivered later in the day/week/month, which is a great productivity tool and means that when I am away from my desk things are still filtering out to my followers, and pages on other platforms are being updated. Hootsuite has a great help function to get you started, with many videos to learn from. If you decide to upgrade to the paid version, which is well worth the few $$ per month, there are plenty of analytics to look at. Use the analytics to monitor what works for you—then do more of what's working for you and drop what isn't working.

Activity 4

Research the platforms and decide which one you like best; then join to familiarise yourself with it.

Listen out for your brand

As people now take to online channels to talk about anything and everything, have you thought about what they may be saying about you or your brand? Twitter is a great tool for listening even if you don't use it for tweeting much. If someone has something negative to say about you or your brand, wouldn't you like to know about it so you can respond? Following are a couple of examples of what I mean.

Real story: get it right — coffee shop

One summer's day I had a bit of spare time in between appointments, so I headed to the nearest coffee shop for a sit-down and a well-earned coffee. I placed my order and took a seat on one of the sofas to watch the world go by down on the waterfront. The sun was streaming in through the windows on a beautiful day, with tourists from all four corners of the world enjoying the day.

As I sat waiting for my drink, my mind wandered from the outside world to what was happening in the coffee shop, or rather what hadn't been happening in the coffee shop. As I took in what I was looking at, I thought I must have been imagining things. The shop front was pretty much glass all the way along, and with the summer sun streaming through it I could really see just how dirty and smeared the windows were. Now, I am not a particularly fussy person when it comes to clean windows, but these were so dirty and smeary that it really did shock me. After all, it was a coffee shop — a place where they serve drinks and food — so to have filthy windows is simply not on.

The coffee shop in question was also part of a large national chain with many coffee shops throughout the country, so you tend to expect a little more than what I was looking at from a reputable brand.

I decided to tweet about it, so I got my iPhone out of my bag and proceeded to tweet where I was, who the coffee chain was and what was bothering me. Within a couple of minutes, one of my followers came back to me and said that they had been in the same coffee shop a couple of days earlier and they too had noticed the same thing, so I wasn't the only one who thought it was below average.

That now made two tweets out there talking about this particular brand's premises in a not-so-flattering way, and others could potentially join in if they were listening and had something to add, but on this occasion, no-one else did.

I thought no more about it as I finished my drink and went to my next appointment, which was a speaking engagement for a client's networking evening, so it was not until a couple of hours later that I received a telephone message left by the CEO of the coffee company. My first thought was, 'Oh my goodness, what have I done?' as I dialled his number. 'What hornet's nest might I have stirred up?'

He was very pleasant and explained that he had seen my tweet and also seen the follow-up tweet from the other person, and was concerned about my experience not being a great one in the coffee shop down the street. He explained that the management of the shop had recently changed and that there were some problems with the glass not being able to be cleaned properly. They were even in discussions with the landlord of the building to see if they could get the glass changed—it was that much of an issue. He assured me they were working on a solution and that my experience was not what he wanted to happen. What else could he do to put matters right?

I wasn't after gift vouchers or anything like that—I just wanted a coffee in a clean environment, but my point is this: he was listening and he acted swiftly to see how he could help. For that, I give the brand top marks. If the company had simply ignored those first tweets, it might have escalated into something bigger because Twitter makes it very easy to shout about things, both good and bad.

I asked him how he had seen the tweet so quickly and he said he had alerts set up on his phone, so again top marks to him for taking an active approach to listening to what is being said about his brand.

Real story: beware of impersonators — HJ Heinz

Back in 2009 Michael decided to see what would happen if he impersonated a big brand on Twitter. He wanted to find out how long he could keep it up before the brand realised they were being impersonated, and what action they would then take. The only criteria for his choice of brand were that they were extremely well known globally, that he had an interest in their brand as he used it himself, and that they didn't already have a social media presence.

He picked on Heinz.

So on 1 December 2009 he set up a Twitter page called @HJ_Heinz, branded it with the Heinz ketchup bottle for a logo, and added a profile informing followers that they could expect news, recipes and information about Heinz. Then he set to work tweeting and getting new followers.

He tweeted interesting information straight from the Heinz website and added links to recipes and anything else he found of interest, but at no time was he ever malicious — that was never the plan. He made sure he was courteous at all times as he was representing a huge global brand. From there, he had to gain followers organically, so he started to search for people who had already mentioned Heinz in their tweets, and followed them.

He also targeted tweeters from the Pittsburgh area, as Heinz is a big part of the community there. It didn't take long to get more than 350 followers, but on 14 December 2009 his account name was changed and he was no longer allowed to carry on as @HJ_Heinz. Twitter notified him that the account was in breach of the Twitter rules and could not continue as it was, and he was also told to take the logo off the page. The name of the account was then changed to @NOTHJ_Heinz. He states in an article about his experiment that no-one from Heinz ever got in touch with him, which was disappointing.

Michael never at any time tried to be malicious; it was simply an experiment for him to see if he could get away with it, which he did for two weeks. So was Heinz really listening every day?

My opinion is that they can't have been, otherwise they would surely have seen the fake account and done something sooner. But another question might be why did they not see Michael as a true fan and see if they could work together in some capacity? He was after all a loyal fan: what better cheerleader does a company need?

This story of how Heinz got caught out is from some time ago but it's still very relevant to many smaller companies today because it's a huge lesson in listening in the right places. You don't hear of big, well-known brands coming up against this sort of thing anymore because, thankfully, they are now all listening and doing something about it if an issue does arise.

Donald Trump has been active on Twitter for a long time, and chose it as his soapbox of choice during the campaign to become president of the United States. He's outspoken, challenging and vocal in his approach, getting into public debates with people from all walks of life. Becoming president has not stopped him. In one tweet, he slammed Nordstrom, where his daughter Ivanka's clothing range was sold, after they decided not to continue selling the range. Nordstrom stock took a dip immediately after the tweet but then bounced back shortly after. Talk about influence. Now that could be the Trump name or the fact that a tweet slamming Nordstrom went viral and shareholders reacted. Influential people are even more influential when you add in a digital soapbox.

Listening online — setting up alerts

So what sort of things should you be listening for and where should you be listening? Twitter is a great place to start, as well as Socialmention, Hootsuite and Google Alerts, which are alerts that are delivered to your inbox about a given keyword such as your company name (these are explained further down). I have set up alerts for Linda Coles, Blue Banana, Blue Bananas, Bluebanana20 and a few others. As most of my social media usernames are bluebanana20, I watch out for both because people often simply refer to me as Blue Banana, and I don't want to miss what they are saying. The problem with this is that I get everything to do with Blue Banana the clothing and body-piercing company. Some of those piercing tweets make my eyes water!

It is an easy job to monitor once you have the systems in place and it only takes me a few seconds a day to filter through the Blue Banana tweets as I've learned to recognise who is who. Set up a column or stream with Hootsuite for the various words or terms you want to listen out for and any tweets containing those words will populate the stream.

You can also listen to what your competitors are saying, even without them knowing that you are listening in, which may be useful in your industry. I used to do this, but found I was spending time worrying about what they were up to rather than concentrating on my own business. If you want to follow someone in your industry, follow someone you admire and can learn from as this is far more positive and probably more worthwhile.

Google Alert

To set a Google Alert, set up a Google account, if you don't have one already, and click on 'alerts' or go to www.google.com/alerts. Depending on how often you want to be informed, you can set the email notifications to 'as it happens', 'daily' or 'weekly', so you can control the number of emails coming in.

If you are watching a search term rather than a word, you will need to put speech marks (" ") around the term. So, for example, if I want to watch out for Blue Banana, I will need to enter "Blue Banana", otherwise I will get alerts with just blue or just banana in them, which is a bit of a waste of time and far too labour-intensive. You can set up as many alerts as you wish and see which ones are of value to you.

Activity 5

Set up your Google Alerts using the keyword ideas below.

Keywords to monitor

Keywords to monitor include:

- your name
- your name spelled incorrectly
- your company name
- your company name abbreviated
- your competitors
- your industry
- topics of interest.

Hootsuite

With Twitter, there are a few ways to monitor tweets, but I find that using Hootsuite and setting up separate streams or columns for each search term is enough. That way, the tweet is quickly filtered out from the main traffic stream and is visibly sitting there in its own column waiting for me to notice it. If you download Hootsuite to your smartphone, you can see the tweets coming through while you are on the move. Again, see which terms you need to monitor as you may find too many a bit of a headache.

The columns can also be used for listening to specific people within your industry or to those you are interested in and want to snoop on.

I also have columns and alerts set up for areas that I want to respond to such as 'looking for a speaker' or 'social media webinar', so I can respond to someone's request quickly. You might do the same for your business. If you are a florist, you might look out for 'florist in Sydney'. Think about what someone tweeting about needing a florist would enter if they're in Sydney—probably something like, 'Can anyone recommend a florist in Sydney?' That would then get picked up and filtered into your column for you to see and pounce on. This is a simple way to use tweets to generate a little extra business.

Activity 6

Set up your streams on Hootsuite using the keyword ideas listed above.

Twitter's advanced search facility

www.twitter.com/search-advanced gives you the same functionality as Hootsuite, but you also have the ability to define the area. As Urgent Couriers found out, having a column set up for 'need a courier' meant that the filter would also pick up tweets from the other side of the world, which was not a lot of good to it. By using www.twitter.com/search-advanced, it could restrict it to within a 100-kilometre radius of Auckland. Much better for its business and it also cuts out the irrelevant tweets.

Real story: local courier uses Twitter to listen

A local courier company, Urgent Couriers, was interviewed on national TV about how it generated business using Twitter and, in particular, how it used the listening tools to help people out. It has also used Twitter to build up its client base by networking—that is, by chatting to other local businesspeople and building a relationship, just like you would offline.

It also has columns set up to filter out its clients' tweets, as well as its prospects' tweets so it can keep up to date with what is going on in their businesses too.

In order to measure its success with spending time on Twitter, it has set up a specific email address so that any emails coming into the company at that address can be tracked back to the success of its Twitter presence. Great idea!

I very nearly missed out on working with a top-five company, but because I had various streams set up listening for me, I caught the conversation before it was too late.

Real story: Using other streams for listening

I was asked if I would be willing to speak about social media at a luncheon for young businesspeople, but it was to be a little different in that it was purely questions and answers over lunch. Not a large gathering, just about 20 people in a private room, which sounded great. I went along on the day, and mixed and mingled with the majority of the guests, but it's hard to get to say hello to everyone, so inevitably there were people I missed. After the lunch was over and I returned to my office I checked Hootsuite as a matter of course, and there were a couple of

(continued)

Real story: Using other streams for listening *(cont'd)*

tweets in my 'Linda Coles' stream, but I did not recognise who had tweeted them. I clicked on her profile and noticed that she worked for one of New Zealand's top-five companies and was simply saying that she had enjoyed the lunch and discussing LinkedIn with me.

Now, she had made the effort to post that, so it warranted a response at the very least, which I did by simply saying something like, 'Glad you found it useful, have a great afternoon'. From that initial conversation on Twitter, we exchanged a handful more tweets over a period of a couple of weeks, and when a complimentary slot became available on a LinkedIn workshop I was running, I offered it to her. To my surprise and delight, she accepted, which meant I was then able to meet her in person and say hi properly.

As time went on, one of her colleagues asked me if I would like to write an article for a new e-magazine that they were launching to all of their business customers in the coming weeks, so obviously I jumped at the chance and our professional relationship grew.

My point here is that without listening for possible tweets, I would never have picked hers up as she had used my name and not my Twitter username. From there, I gently kept the conversation going, which resulted in her attending a workshop I was running so she was able to see the depth of my knowledge on the subject and then pass my details on to a colleague for the article submission.

To be able to work with one of the country's top-five companies is a real honour and would have been almost impossible without Twitter.

Conclusion of chapter 4

Twitter can be used for many different business tasks as well as keeping up to date with your interests, but at least set it up as a listening post and check in regularly to see what, if anything, is being said about you or your brand.

Each day, spend five minutes in the morning posting relevant and interesting information, and revisit Twitter in the afternoon to see if you have any replies that need attention.

Your content plan will come in very handy when using Twitter so make sure you have filled in all of the boxes.

CHAPTER 5
YouTube

Key areas we will cover in chapter 5:

✓ why you should create a video

✓ some real examples of smaller businesses that use video

✓ setting up a YouTube channel

✓ making your video

✓ uploading your video.

Video marketing is fast becoming a popular way to explain a product or service, and sites such as YouTube are very popular. Think of YouTube as a resource channel to find the answer to your question, as well as an entertainment centre for funny videos.

Quick facts on YouTube

Here are some interesting YouTube facts:

▶ It was founded in 2005.

▶ It has 30 million visitors per day.

▶ Five billion videos are watched per day.

▶ Eighty per cent of traffic is from outside the United States.

▶ Fifty per cent of the time it is watched on a mobile phone.

Why create a video?

It's that exposure word again. How great would it be if one of your videos had millions of views worldwide and everyone was talking about your brand? And all for the cost of making a great video?

But in order for a video to go viral and be shared across the world, you need to really home in on emotion. Your video needs to be either very funny, sad, loving or any other emotion you want to use, but the key is emotion: pull on the viewers' heartstrings or laughter strings. Think back to the points from Jonah Berger's book, *Contagious*: it's that emotional factor, the thing that quickens your pulse that makes someone share.

We've all received emails in our inbox with links to funny videos — from funny home movies and footage of cats, to funny commercials and professional training videos. The common denominator is that they are all funny.

When you see a funny video, you are more likely to pass it on to your friends or post it to your Facebook wall for all to see. Imagine if you are Heineken, and your series of funny commercials is being passed around from one person's network to another: the exposure you get from that could be massive, and the only expense is the cost of the video. If you aim that video content at your target market at the same time, it's hard to lose. The trick is to make something good enough that people *want to share*.

As our lives get busier, our attention span starts to wane a little, so a short, sharp video explaining something you need to understand is another great way of accessing information. I no longer use the 'help' function in Word or Excel: if I want to learn how to put a column into a spreadsheet, for example, I go to YouTube, type in the search terms I need, and pick a quick video to show me how to do it. It really suits my style of learning, as it does many others' too: if I can see how something is done, rather than read about it, it is much clearer and quicker for me to understand.

It would be great if your videos went viral and achieved massive exposure, but in reality very few do. But you do need to aim for your video to be passed around, and even if you don't get to the millions of views, the more people who see what you have created, the more people who are aware of your product or service.

What are people watching?

There has been a definite shift in which videos get the really big viewer numbers. It's no longer the lost dog that gets found, or the silly antics a cat gets up to when its owner isn't looking, but the music videos. We have had music videos for many years now, but they really do seem to have taken off for the top artists. Indeed, at the time of writing, the top 10 videos by views include Bruno Mars, Taylor Swift, PSY and Justin Bieber. But it's 'Gangnam Style' from PSY that takes the top spot with nearly three *billion* views — a video loaded back in 2012 and still going strong. There are only two in the top 10 that are not music-related videos and they are both children's videos (I guess it's easy to play them from a mobile device).

Rather than the hordes of videos that used to circulate on any particular topic in the past — most of which no-one had time to watch — it seems that these days there are 'star' ones that stand out. For example, if you are really interested in cycling, there will be a hot video doing the rounds in the cycling genre.

Every year, ad agencies in the United States are tasked with creating the most entertaining ads possible for airing during the Super Bowl commercial breaks. The mainly 30-second spots are probably the most expensive in the world because of the many millions of viewers watching the match — and especially the latest ad creations, which the Super Bowl has become famous for. The ads are analysed in depth, including what has worked, and what has not, and why. Indeed, Mashable publishes the best of the Super Bowl ads and how they are trending pretty much as they happen. We are even starting to see ad teasers, which the big brands use to test the water and gauge viewers' reactions before the launch of the full-size ad on the big day, in the hope it will be the best ad. This is quite a clever way to start people talking about your brand and, if you have the budget to do so, make adjustments to the longer version, or scrap it altogether and start afresh if you need to. Big money is at stake to get it absolutely right during such a popular sporting highlight of the year.

Real story: Blendtec annihilates to show its strength

Back in 2010, a regular household name in food blenders, Blendtec, was looking for something a little more innovative to catch its audience's eye and gain valuable exposure at the same time. Why not see what the blender can successfully blend? A whole series of videos was created over a period of time demonstrating different items being blended, with the most popular item being the iPhone. With a channel creating videos with over 250 million views of the 'mad professor'—who was in fact the founder of Blendtec, Tom Dickson—blending items such as the iPhone to dust, Blendtec's name and sales quickly skyrocketed. The series of 'will it blend' videos blends all kinds of things, such as boxes of matches, a camcorder, Bic lighters and the iPhone 7. Dickson even blended what he termed as 'Hillary Clinton's emails' on a smartphone in a stunt on TV around election time, as well as Obama's golf club. The series is so popular you can buy T-shirts with the slogan 'Tom Dickson is my homeboy' on them. After many more different blending attempts, the videos still go on today, probably making the Blendtec channel one of the oldest running and most successful.

Examples of smaller businesses that use video

Frog Recruitment has used videos to fill positions that are a bit out of the norm with great success. Take a look at 'MOTAT career video', which was produced to show what goes on in a transport museum on a daily basis and to introduce the rest of the team to a potential new employee—a low-cost way to create a bit of a buzz, fill a position and promote a great cause at the same time. Maybe you could use this approach to fill an exciting or unique position at your company?

John Spence, author and business-improvement expert, regularly uses videos to review business books: a great way to show his expertise as a business writer, gain more valuable exposure to his own personal brand and add value to the tribe that follows him in the business world. If John says a book is good, it usually is. I regularly visit his site to watch his short, informative videos. What could you review to gain that sort of exposure?

Tony Vidler, an adviser to the financial advice industry, has created a whole series of 'Top Tips': very short and succinct video tips aimed at financial advisers to help them grow their own businesses. They tend to be about a minute long and are top-and-tailed with his logo and contact details, great for when someone shares one. He releases them at regular intervals to keep his brand on people's radars and add some value at the same time.

Corning Glass created a couple of popular videos about how glass will feature in our future. It's a very technical product, but the videos are presented as a cross between looking to the future and what we can already see happening now with things such as glass mobile phones and cooktops.

Video ideas

Some simple ideas for your video:

- a welcome message on your website
- information about the future of your product
- a description of the problem your product solves
- a demonstration of your product
- your current TV ads
- an insider's view of your business
- industry tips
- event footage with testimonials
- a project unfolding to completion
- new product launches
- holiday wishes.

Making your video

Many people's first thoughts about making a video are, 'What will it cost, what equipment will I need and what should I do in the video in the first place?'

The first part of the question is easy enough to answer as the cost of creating a video can run from a handful of dollars to many thousands, so it really depends on your budget and what you want to achieve. With video tools now so readily available, even if you don't own a video camera yourself, you may know someone you can borrow one from.

Some benefits of using video:

▶ You can explain a technical product easily.

▶ You can add personality to your product.

▶ Viewers can meet the team.

▶ It has the ability to be passed around for greater exposure.

▶ It's relatively cheap.

The content of the video is a little more complicated and I will give you some more ideas of what others are doing later in the chapter.

Your equipment is important, but it doesn't need to be film-industry high-definition standard that costs the earth: you can now get some very good small cameras that will do the job perfectly well—including smartphones—and there are many low-cost options on the market. I would look out for one that will allow you to use a microphone with it because you may be forgiven for bad lighting, but you'll *never* be forgiven for bad audio. If viewers can't hear you, they won't stick around to watch the rest of your video.

With regard to the lighting, natural is always best, with the light shining on your face rather than on the back of your head if you are presenting, but do a dummy run first to check if you need to make any adjustments.

Most cameras will record for a couple of hours on a full battery, which is ample to get the shots you need, but you will need to then edit your video, which is not as hard as you might think. If you use a PC or laptop, you more than likely have Windows Movie Maker already installed, and if you are on a Mac, you will have iMovie. The first time I put a short movie together it took me a couple of hours to figure it out, but the second one was finished in just a few minutes and I used YouTube's resources to do it. I simply put into the search box what I was looking to do with Movie Maker, such as add music, and watched the video.

You can even add in a branded first slide and credits at the end if you so wish. Don't forget to add your company details so people can get hold of you.

Activity 1

Start practising with your video editing software on your computer to see how easy it is! Find a video on YouTube to show you how to use your software if you are unsure.

Following are some things you should think about when making your video.

Length

The optimum length of a video has dropped to about 30 seconds, which is, surprisingly, ample time for you to get your message across. The first five seconds of any video are the most important part and you will really need to grab the viewers' attention in this time if you want them to watch the rest of your video. Dive straight in, otherwise you will find people switching off in droves, as we just don't have the time available that we used to have.

If you are making a series such as a short TV show that you are planning to do regularly, about eight minutes is your maximum. Unless you are interviewing a really special person, videos of 30 minutes or more are long gone, so bear this in mind when you plan your video. For a video interview, stick to about 10 to 15 minutes.

Content

Think about what you want to achieve in the first place. Is it to create a short series of value-added videos to share with your clients and prospects, or is it more about brand exposure and creating a funny video that you hope will get noticed and go viral? Of course, there is no point making a video that is not going to be passed on, so even if it is an educational video, make it so content-rich that others will find it beneficial and want to pass it on.

Air New Zealand has made a series of award-winning light-hearted safety videos and has realised that by keeping them current, relevant, amusing and updated, more travellers will pay attention and watch the serious message they contain. They can all be seen on YouTube; many have amassed millions of views.

Interviews are an easy way to add flavour to your site so consider who in your industry would be willing to share their expertise with you. Think about industry experts, famous people you are connected to in some way, people of interest in general, or the lighter side of your company's management team—but make it interesting and content-rich.

Some YouTube video-making dos and don'ts

Do:

- use a microphone
- consider your lighting (not too light or dark)
- reduce background noise
- decide on a content plan for a series of videos
- create videos regularly, whether that be monthly or quarterly.

Don't:

- ever upload video you do not have the rights for, such as concert footage
- ever add distasteful content; read the terms and conditions if you are unsure
- infringe copyright
- leave negative comments
- make it too long—viewers will turn it off.

Activity 2

Brainstorm what content you could put into a series of videos.

Setting up your YouTube channel and uploading your video

Once you have shot and edited your video and are happy with it, the obvious place to post it is YouTube, so set yourself up an account, or 'channel'. Your account name should be your business name if it is not already taken, and there is space to fill out a bit more information on the profile, so make use of that.

You can customise your channel's look with images by clicking on the 'customise channel' link in 'settings'—and while you are there, click on 'activity sharing' and fill out your Twitter and Facebook details and what you would like to share. This is another easy step to utilise so when you upload a new video, mark a video as a favourite or 'like' a video it will automatically update your network for you.

Activity 3

Set up your YouTube channel and customise the page with your brand colours.

Uploading

To upload a new video, click on 'upload' and follow the simple instructions. Your video can be in a range of formats, be up to 128 GB in size and have a maximum duration of 11 hours. If your video is longer than 15 minutes, you will have to verify your account by following some simple steps. Once your account is verified, you will then be able to upload the longer file. Uploading takes a few minutes, so you can fill out the rest of the information while you are waiting.

You will be asked for:

▶ *A title.* This needs to accurately reflect what the video is about but it also needs to contain keywords. I usually add the title followed by my name or company name, depending on the available space.

▶ *A description.* What is the video about? Get those keywords in there too. You want your video to be found easily by others typing in relevant search criteria.

▶ *Tags.* Tags are simply the main keywords about your video's content. This is how people will find your video so it is important they are accurate.

▶ *Category and privacy preferences.* These are self-explanatory; you just need to choose what options best suit your needs. If you want everyone to be able to see your video, select the public setting. You can keep a video private if you are not quite happy with it and want to edit it later.

Where can I post it?

When your video is uploaded fully you can begin promoting it. There are plenty of places to promote your video or video channel. Here are a few ideas:

▶ Load it up to www.vimeo.com.

▶ Post it to your blog.

▶ Add it to Pinterest.

▶ Post it to your Facebook page (as an upload or as a link).

▶ Embed it on your website.

▶ Add it to your email signature (linked to your channel).

▶ Include it in your electronic newsletter.

- ▶ Tweet the link via Twitter.

- ▶ Upload it to your rich media section on LinkedIn.

- ▶ Set up a Slideshare account and upload it there too.

Promoting your video

YouTube is owned by Google, so you can promote your video just like you can with Google AdWords, and you can see examples of this all over the YouTube site. Companies both large and small can make use of it depending on their budget and you will very often see some of the big brands promoting their product across the video you are about to watch. You can link your YouTube account to your AdWords account to promote your views to others. (More on AdWords in chapter 13.)

Subscribing to other channels

By clicking the 'subscribe' button on someone else's channel, you will be notified when they have uploaded a video, but you will also find that if you subscribe to theirs, they may well return the favour and subscribe back. That means they are notified when you upload another video, so you are creating another set of connections to communicate with.

Quick tip

Don't just stop at one video; try to create a regular series, even if it's only twice per year.

Conclusion of chapter 5

Videos really do give your business another tool to make use of in many different ways, and once you have made a couple successfully, you will no doubt get the bug to make more and more. You could be pleasantly surprised at how your customers and prospects receive your great new videos.

Look back at your content plan and see how you thought videos could be a part of it. Hopefully you now have some very clear ideas about how you can use them creatively.

CHAPTER 6
Instagram

Key areas we will cover in chapter 6:

✓ using Instagram in your business

✓ posting with Instagram tools

✓ creating Instagram videos

✓ getting followers on Instagram

✓ advertising on Instagram

✓ some Instagram success stories.

Instagram provides you with another set of image, GIF and video sharing tools, enabling you to create and edit great footage and images to share on your other social media sites, as well as on Instagram. It's even become a Snapchat competitor thanks to Instagram Stories and Instagram Live. Add in its 'save' feature and it takes on Pinterest too.

Quick facts on Instagram

Here are some interesting Instagram facts:

▶ It has an even split of male and female users.

▶ There are over 600 million monthly active users.

▶ There are 400 million daily users.

▶ Instagram was bought by Facebook in 2012.

What is Instagram?

Instagram is the best image-sharing app on your device, enabling you to add creative filters to both photos and video. For example, when you have taken a photo, you can choose one of the clever filter options or editing tools to make the image black and white, sepia, old fashioned, brighter and much more—whatever takes your fancy. These images can then be shared with your friends via both Facebook and Twitter. You can also post via email so you can either send a copy to someone or post it to yourself for filing elsewhere.

Although Instagram does not directly offer the option to repost other people's videos and photos to your account, there are many apps available that will link to Instagram and make reposting possible. One of the best and most popular repost apps currently available is Repost for Instagram.

People can comment on your posts and you can also add a link to your website in the description just to encourage click-throughs to your brand. It's worth mentioning that hashtags rule on Instagram, probably even more so than on Twitter. Many people simply use the hashtags as the description, which seems to be quite acceptable. While you can use up to 30 (yes, 30!) hashtags, I think that's overkill—but you decide.

Many social media channels, and Facebook in particular, are using more and more images, so creating your own with easy filters means you can really post something far superior than a random stock image. It is much more personal and creative. It also has an ad platform that is accessible via Facebook, as Instagram is owned by Facebook, so once your ads are set there, they filter through if you've asked for them to.

Using Instagram in your business

Brands are now encouraging their customers to take Instagram pictures of themselves in the brand's clothes or with the brand's product in some way, usually by way of a competition. Take a look at Nasty Gal's Instagram site (www.instagram.com/nastygal) to see some of these. By asking the consumer to use the hashtag #nastygal, they are able to find them all and collate them for their own marketing purposes. Generally, part of the terms and conditions of the competition is that by using the designated hashtag, people are giving the brand permission to use the images. As most people who enter would love to see their name or their works of art in lights, it's not usually a problem and so everyone wins. Nasty Gal also uses Olapic (www.olapic.com) as a way of accessing these images.

If you want to feed your business Facebook page directly from Instagram when you share initially, be sure to set up a business profile; otherwise it will post to your personal profile page by default.

Real story: Ben & Jerry's capture euphoria

Ice-cream brand Ben & Jerry's ran a similar competition to Nasty Gal's by using the hashtag #captureeuphoria. Viewers were asked to post their Instagram pictures with their version of euphoria. They could include the ice-cream brand or not; it didn't matter—they just wanted a great feel-good campaign. The winning Instagram images were then used in Ben & Jerry's printed advertising such as billboards, bus-stop posters and other marketing media in the local area of each winner, with a total of 25 winners in all. Imagine the winners' surprise when they picked up a magazine from their local store and their Instagram picture of euphoria was printed there. A really great feel-good campaign for both sides. Let your customers do the work for you and create great content for your brand, as well as having some fun doing it.

Activity 1

Create your Instagram account and link it to your other social sites ready for posting great content.

Instagram tools

Instagram has various tools available for different types of posts. Stories, Zoom and Live have come about from other platforms and been incorporated into Instagram because they have proven popular.

Instagram Stories

It was Snapchat that started the 'in-the-moment' idea and Instagram has taken it a step further. You now don't need to worry about over-posting because you can add all your daily activity, photos and videos into a file — essentially a story but in a slideshow format. These stories from people you follow are displayed in the bar along the top of your screen, and disappear after 24 hours. You can tap them to send as private messages, but with stories there is no public liking or comments. Depending on the privacy setting of your account, your stories will be public or private. They don't need to be professionally shot because they vanish, and it's a great way for brands to experiment and see what works before investing money in the idea. As stories are always displayed at the top of the feed screen, it means they are much more visible to the viewer, so it's a great tool to make the most of. There are no in-depth analytics for stories. One big brand that's doing well is Jamie Oliver's Instagram page, 'Jamie's food tube'. Have a look at www.instagram.com/jamiesfoodtube, follow it and keep an eye on how it uses Instagram Stories.

Instagram Zoom

This tool allows users to zoom in on photos and videos, so if your product has plenty of detail, such as a fine detail on a garment or artwork, this is the way to display it. Likewise, it works well for great food pictures or if you have a post with lots of text.

Instagram Live

Instagram Live is featured first in the stories line-up so it is extremely prominent. If you don't have the budget to spend on ads, use Live as a way to get in front, though you need to do it often because once the broadcast is over, it disappears from the app (however, you could save a copy to your device just for safe-keeping). This is different from Facebook Live, which keeps a recording intact with comments and likes attached. If you use Live, decide whether you want comments or not because you can turn them off. To start an Instagram Live broadcast, tap on the Your Story profile photo (with the + sign next to it) at the top of your Instagram newsfeed and click 'live'. You can use it to launch a new product, make an announcement, do a live Q&A session or for other impromptu events.

Instagram videos

Instagram videos can use the same filter system as photos, making your 60-second videos look hip and quite different from something you shot with your video camera on your phone. Another advantage of using the Instagram video app is that it does also populate your Instagram page on your desktop, so you can see the videos all in one handy place that is bigger than your mobile screen. Many brands that run competitions where you enter by submitting a video ask that you use Instagram as opposed to any other camera or software program because the entrant is then limited to 60 seconds, so everyone starts on a level playing field. These can be emailed to the competition email address for you to see and decide on a winner. There are also plenty of apps available to make it easy to download, upload and do all sorts of other things with videos, and new apps seem to pop up every week, so see what suits your needs. Find one for what you need via Google.

Getting followers on Instagram

As for all platforms, you want followers, likes and comments wherever possible and Instagram is no exception. Even though content can't be shared, you still want to know your efforts are worthwhile and doing the job you intended—building a relationship. So what are the best ways to get more followers?

▶ *Have a theme.* This goes back to your content strategy at the beginning of the book and it should be a given, but you can break themes down a little. Say your subject for February is 'heart health month'. Your theme within that could be healthy fruit and vegetables, which easily lend themselves to great image creation and messages.

▶ *Keep it visual.* Take the best shots, add the best filters and create something special.

▶ *Add a description that's worth it.* This is your space to talk about the image so tell a story and add some hashtags.

▶ *Include hashtags.* Use a few of each, branded ones and unbranded ones.

▶ *Post consistently.* Do it daily where you can, but whatever schedule you choose, stick to it.

Activity 2

What themes can you incorporate into your plan?

Instagram ads

While you can't create an ad campaign on Instagram, you can create one through Facebook. Just be sure to choose 'Instagram' when you decide where you want the ad to be placed. Do remember you can't upload a video longer than 60 seconds as an ad because Instagram can't run them. You can identify an ad because it will have 'sponsored' at the top of the post.

What's popular on Instagram?

So just what are the best posts—ever?

▶ Beyoncé's pregnancy picture of 2017 has over 10 million likes.

▶ Selena Gomez and a Coke bottle with her lyrics on it has 6 million likes.

▶ Taylor Swift has various pictures running in the millions.

Celebrities will always take centre stage on the platforms as besotted fans lap up their every move, but there is plenty of room for all of us so don't worry if you don't have Selena Gomez in your corner holding your product. In a conversation with a client, she told me she hardly spent any time at all on Facebook, preferring instead to scroll through Instagram because she felt it is a more positive experience. You rarely see people ranting and raving on Instagram like you do on Facebook so maybe she's onto something.

Instagram success stories

I asked a designer and bag manufacturer how they use Instagram so successfully. This is what they said.

Real story: Cora + Spink bag it

Cora + Spink, founded by Tim Johnson in 2015 in Bromsgrove, England, weave 24-ounce canvas, tan the leather, cast the hardware and cut and triple stitch each panel by hand to make the best bags you will ever carry. When you need a bag, backpack or duffle for the commute to work, travel or studies, and you need that bag to last. We have that bag for you. And every bag we sell is limited edition. Once they're gone — they're gone!

And that means each product has a story.

This is the message we wanted to get across in our marketing from day one — Tim, the founder, who is so incredibly passionate about his work, regularly says, 'I can't *wait* to get out of bed each day and get working'. He has a background in fashion and product development and always knew he wanted to set up his own fashion line.

The beginnings

We started out with no website, no social media and a handful of customers. We now have 1359 followers on Instagram, 683 followers on Twitter and many likes on Facebook — all organic, so they are all genuinely interested in our product. We've never bought 'fake' followers like many companies do!

We knew social media was the way to go to reach our audience. We love taking pictures, we love our bags, and we love what we do, so why wouldn't we use it? It's cool, it's trendy and it fits with what we're about!

When we go out each day, we always take pictures — whether they be styled with one of our bags in them or just a picture that says what we're about. We want our customers to relate to what we do — to fall in love with our bags, our values and think the same things are as funny as we do, such as ducks in a pond, cats climbing up the curtains or doing a dance.

We wanted to avoid mass marketing and have a bit more of a strategic focus with social media, creating desirable, quality products with an intangible, emotional appeal so you can really hear the voice of Cora + Spink.

The aim is to create products that are attractive, funky, a bit different—bags filled with a consistent quality as we're aiming for repeat business. Customers choose to buy a Cora + Spink bag time after time—this repeat business is evident through the engagement from customers with their comments on our Instagram page. Instagram for business gives us the insights to modify and tweak campaigns daily. We've witnessed that the time of day we choose for posting is important too. We don't use bots or automated systems—everything we do is done by ourselves. We are small and independent and our budget is tight—we don't have the big bucks like our competitors.

Reach and engagement

The desire for engagement and response in social media is the driving force for any marketing campaign. Although small and with minimal budget, we've managed to capture an audience that is keen and willing to like and share our Instagram feed.

With many of our posts, our engagement is ridiculously high. Take for example our post at Hermosa Beach where reach impressions were 185; 142 of those were unique, and we had 146 engagements. It's a goal to achieve these figures—almost unrealistic—however, it demonstrates the difference between genuine organic followers as opposed to 'fake' followers who aren't truly engaged.

The Instagram feed shares stories with real people—friends, family and customers send us photos using the bags on their travels, creating an emotional appeal. It goes back to the saying often attributed to Carl W. Buehner. 'They may forget what you said—but they will never forget how you made them feel.' It's the same with our brand. It's all about

(continued)

Real story: Cora + Spink bag it *(cont'd)*

the emotional attachment and that's what we hope comes across with our social marketing and the whole marketing orientation of Cora + Spink. Everyone we meet loves the bags!

The appeal is evident for us all to see, through word of mouth and with repeat business proving time after time it is one of our key successes to date. The creative use of hashtags reinforces our friends', families' and customers' love of their bags along with ours—we want our personality to shine through! We've seen that choosing the right hashtags has an impact on engagement.

We like local. We've recently teamed up with local band The Fidgets for some joint promotional work, with the band promoted through social media. This has mutual benefit, widening the reach of our posts and increasing engagement with our followers and theirs.

We focus on storytelling of our travels, of our adventures—after all, that's what 'Spink' means in Bengali: 'flight'—whether it be a trip to the seaside, holidays to LA, Greece, Iceland, Italy or South America, or city breaks to London. Our friends and family are lucky enough to travel to beautiful places.

We know that customers don't like the direct sell. It's about the brand story and brand connection, which is what we are all about. Word of mouth goes a long way, so we reckon if we can get this right and if we win the hearts and minds of the customer too, then many more people across the world will enjoy our bags of joy!

You can follow us at www.coraandspink.co.uk.

What Cora + Spink have done is extremely visually appealing as well as incredibly simple. It proves you don't need a pro photographer—just have an imagination and a decent camera on your smartphone.

Here's another story worth sharing. This is how Julie went from zero to 16 000 Instagram followers in just 18 months!

Real story: Julie — 0 to 16 000 in 18 months

There comes a time in all our lives when we have the choice to embrace change or fight against it. While I had enjoyed being a stay-at-home mum and having run my own business, I felt destined for more. When my eldest son went off to university I knew there would never be a better time to focus on myself and my career.

I've always loved helping people, so at the age of 45 I decided to follow my passion and qualify as a life and business coach. Having run a business before, I knew that being a technical expert in your industry wasn't enough. I realised that I would have to focus on getting clients if I wanted to grow a thriving coaching practice. While I wasn't particularly active on social media at the time I could see the huge potential it had when it comes to marketing your business. I also liked the idea of coaching internationally and felt that social media was the best way to connect with people all around the world.

I initially started on Facebook by creating a business page, but found myself getting frustrated with the lack of engagement—especially that only a small number of people would see your posts because of the way Facebook's algorithm works. So I decided to try Instagram. I wasn't disappointed; I loved the type of content that was being shared on Instagram. It really helped me start my day on a positive note. I also liked the fact that you could easily search for your ideal clients and connect with them.

When I first started out on Instagram I struggled to get followers and I didn't get much engagement on my posts. I didn't get disheartened though because I started making some good connections almost immediately by reaching out and connecting with people.

(continued)

Real story: Julie—0 to 16 000 in 18 months *(cont'd)*

As time went on I became even more hooked. I decided I wanted to learn as much as I could about social media, and Instagram in particular. I followed what some of the top experts in the industry were doing and started taking courses. Once I started putting into practice what I'd learned, the engagement increased. My number of followers began to grow and I was getting new leads every week. Part of what makes Instagram great is the willingness of people to engage in a conversation. It's these personal connections that I love and aim for. It's also these personal connections that I've found convert into long-term fans and customers.

I'm often asked how I grew my following to over 16 000 in 18 months. Fans and followers are one thing. Having people who genuinely engage with you and your content is quite different. First of all, growing a community of people who love what you share enough to like and comment on your posts doesn't happen overnight.

Here are a few things you can do that will make a massive difference to your growth and your ability to convert followers into paying clients.

- *Choose your username and display name wisely.* These are searchable so think about what your ideal client might search for if they were looking for you. It's also a good idea to have your name in here so that people can connect with you on a personal level.

- *Create a rocking bio.* Here you want to tell people what you do and what they will see if they follow you. Use emojis and add a bit of personality.

- *Have a very clear identity by using brand colours and themed content.*

- *Choose your hashtags wisely.* Use a mix of popular hashtags (100 000+) and less popular ones (over 1000). That way you will not only get your image in front of a lot of people, but it will also stay in the explore feed a bit longer. It's not worth using hashtags if they only have a few posts, unless it's a unique hashtag for your business.

- *Don't just wait for people to find you.* Search for and engage with your ideal client's content.

- *Be wary of automated software.* There are apps that automate following, liking and commenting on other people's feeds. These breach Instagram's terms and could result in your account being suspended. The engagement is fake and most people can spot it, and as such you are unlikely to reach your marketing objectives.

- *Use instant messages to build relationships.* Used correctly, instant messages are a great way to initiate a conversation and build a connection. Send messages that show you are not just interested in pushing your products or services but that you are actually interested in talking. When the time is right for a sales discussion, see if you can set up a phone call with them or send them to your website. Conversations work better when they take place across channels.

If you think you can just push out content and everyone is going to come running, you're sadly mistaken. Social media works best when you focus on building relationships with your ideal clients, so you are going to need to find and check out their content too. It takes time and consistency, but it's worth the effort. I'm always looking to connect with new people. If you'd like to connect with me you can do that at Instagram.com/lifecoachjulie.

Conclusion of chapter 6

Instagram is a winner and will be around for a long while to come because it's so simple and users love it. If users are using it, brands find ways to catch and engage with them—which is just what you and your business need to do. There is plenty of space to stand out wherever your prospective customers hang out online; you just have to capture their attention.

CHAPTER 7
Pinterest

Key areas we will cover in chapter 7:

✓ setting up a Pinterest page

✓ explaining pins and boards

✓ getting great images

✓ exploring business board ideas

✓ using Pinterest for content on other platforms.

Scrapbooking has long been the hobby of many so it makes sense that there is an electronic version of the popular pastime for the twenty-first century—it's called Pinterest.

Quick facts on Pinterest

Here are some interesting Pinterest facts:

▶ It was launched in 2010.

▶ It has approximately 150 million active users.

▶ Eighty-five per cent of pinners are female.

▶ Eighty million users are outside the United States.

▶ It's online scrapbooking.

▶ It can be linked to other social sites.

▶ There is a mobile app available.

Online scrapbooking made simple

The beauty of the digital version of scrapbooking is that everyone can see your scrapbooks if you have your privacy settings set as public, allowing you to share your favourite things for all to see. If you are a bricks-and-mortar store that sells products, this is another great option you can use to ensure more people see what you have to offer, particularly if you have a dreamy photogenic product such as food, design or fashion.

The secret to Pinterest success is sharing great images for others—and yourself—to admire and dream about. Imagine being able to gaze at perfect images of food, travel destinations, wedding dresses, fast cars, fashion and more—whatever your interests are.

In fact, any product that produces beautiful images and allows someone to dream will work on Pinterest. You can become a curator of your niche or product, drive traffic back to your main website, find like-minded people with your content and develop your own online profile within your field on Pinterest.

What is a pin?

Every image that you post to your Pinterest page, either directly from your computer or from a website, is a pin. When someone likes what you have posted they pass it on by reposting, or repinning, it to their own boards. You pin images onto boards instead of into a physical scrapbook—and that's about it for the jargon side of Pinterest.

You don't have to spend a fortune buying images, though. You can instantly pin images from websites as you see them. This can be done either by clicking on a 'pin it' button downloaded to your browser bar, or by clicking the 'pin it' buttons that appear alongside an image on a site you may be visiting. You can now commonly see the Facebook 'like' button doing a similar job. These little sharing calls to action are much more commonplace today than ever before, so the more of these prompts you have on your own main website to encourage others to share your product images, the better it is for you.

Setting up your Pinterest page

Let's have a look at the mechanics of setting up your own Pinterest profile and boards.

Create your profile

You can create either a personal or a business page, depending on what you want from your page. I have created a combination personal and business page because I am Blue Banana, so it makes sense for me to drive traffic to one place rather than two. My page is called 'Blue Banana 20 — Linda Coles' so anyone looking for either name will find it.

Enter the basic information in the boxes as you go, making sure to add in your website as well as links to your other social channels. The more you can cross-share your content, the better, allowing others to find your other social channels easily. Add your profile picture — and that's about it.

Activity 1

Set up your Pinterest page. Find interesting boards from others that you admire and follow them, both for learning and finding great content to share.

Create some boards

Think outside the box for your board names: get creative as well as obvious. For instance, you might split your travel boards into 'places I have been', 'places I want to visit' and 'places I would like to get married' and so on, thereby creating three very different boards on a similar subject.

If you are in the business-to-business (B2B) sector, like me, it can be tricky to come up with board names for your industry that contain great images, so I have created some called 'cool blue things' (obviously because of Blue Banana): 'I aspire to meet...' and 'inspirational quotes' as well as boards on social media and building relationships. There are also more personal boards such as fashion I like and shoes (of course). When I write novels, I start a board and add my characters or destinations for easy reference to flick back to. I also have a book cover board with various designs pinned to it.

Pinterest is certainly more relevant to some industries than others. Here are a few really good examples of great boards:

► www.pinterest.com/wholefoods

► www.pinterest.com/gap

► www.pinterest.com/gucci

► www.pinterest.com/nordstrom

► www.pinterest.com/pretzelcrisps.

They all have great photos and are all very dream-worthy—just what Pinterest is about—and there are also some quite quirky board ideas. I particularly like the Pretzel Crisps Genius Life Hacks board www.pinterest.com/pretzelcrisps/genius-life-hacks because it is really helpful information for around the home.

Think about some of the boards you would like to keep for yourself—nothing to do with your business, but a place to store your dreams and aspirations, your secret plans and your bright ideas. They don't all have to be public boards; you can make private ones too, as well as public ones that you can share with nominated people. For instance, in developing my last book cover, I pinned some ideas to a board named 'book cover ideas' and shared it with my publisher so she could see my thoughts and add her own in too, making it a collaboration while at the same time allowing everyone else to see them. With secret boards, you can invite certain others to view them, which is really useful if you are planning your wedding and you don't want the groom to see what you are planning but you do want your future sister-in-law to be able to see and perhaps contribute.

Whatever you name your boards, make the headings short and relevant, including a keyword if possible. You want the whole board name to show rather than ending in '...', use no more than 20 characters, including spaces.

You can also rearrange your boards in order so that when visitors land on your Pinterest page for the first time, your best or most relevant boards show up top. Likewise, the main image on each board can be changed to the best one, with the others displayed along the bottom. First impressions matter.

Some business board ideas:

- seasonal
- events
- core values
- trends
- team members
- offers
- tutorials
- videos
- just because.

Pinning

You can find content to share from the search function or from the drop-down menu on your profile page. You will find pictures on just about everything possible, apart from pornography, which is a definite no-no. Anything from animals to women's fashion; there is even a popular section to see what is hot right now. Some of these images have been pinned thousands of times: imagine if you were the generator of that image, perhaps from your own website. What great exposure for you!

While I am writing this I am skipping between Pinterest and writing and I have just re-pinned a delicious-looking lemon, Greek yoghurt and cream cheese cake that has caught my eye. The nice thing about it is that the whole recipe on how to make the cake is attached, as well as the pin creator's name and comments from others. Once I have pinned it, another option pops up and that is to embed the whole image and recipe onto my own website, linking back again to the originator. Now, if I was in the food business, I might do it, but it's not going to work on a website about digital marketing. Shame! If, on the other hand, you were in the food business, you could create a whole page on your main website devoted to dreamy food pins to make your own site even more appealing, or turn your favourite board into a banner image running across a web page that updates when you add new pins, all by adding a short piece of code to your website.

But you don't have to just re-pin from boards already on Pinterest: you can pin great images as you find them on other websites. The ultimate way is to create your own image and get others to re-pin it, or pass it on. Like all social media sites, the developers are constantly updating and changing functionality so I won't discuss image sizes because they will probably change. I think it is safe, however, to say that long images (portrait) work better than wide images (landscape) because the board shape suits them better, so stick to long and slim where possible.

Make sure you use keywords relevant to your pin in the description box to enable others who are searching to find your work. Note that hashtags only really work as the keyword, not the actual hashtag as on Twitter (where it originated from), so don't clutter the description with them. They do, however, serve as a sort of shorthand for what the content is about; for example, #lovevalentines tells me it's about Valentine's Day.

Adding the price of a product into the description is also a good idea as there is no other place to put it, unless you add it to the image, which would look a bit messy. After all, the image is the important hook to make you want more.

Pinning strategy

Like everything you do on social media, you need to incorporate pinning into your main marketing plan to be consistent and effective, so decide what you will pin and when.

A few things to consider with regard to your pinning content strategy:

▶ Pin consistently rather than in bursts then drought periods.

▶ Pin from different sources.

▶ Pin original content where possible.

▶ Decide on keywords that need to be incorporated into your descriptions.

▶ Use images on your website for others to pin from.

▶ Re-pin others' original content and comment on it where possible.

Activity 2
Set up at least two boards, and start adding pins to your boards.

Pinning etiquette

Pins, re-pins, commenting and liking all carry the same etiquette as on all the other sites: just be your normal, friendly self and thank others for contributing to your pins or respond to others' comments as applicable, just as you would if someone was interacting with you in reality.

Conclusion of chapter 7

Pinning is great fun as well as a great tool for many businesses, particularly fashion and food-based ones! It's also a great place to put things to review later, such as articles that you come across, and I now have boards packed with things to do or read later!

If you post great images, not just good ones, you are on the right track. Happy pinning.

CHAPTER 8
Snapchat

Sweta Patel is an expert on Snapchat so it made sense to include a chapter from her in this book. You can find out more about her expertise at her website, www.globalmarketingtactics.com.

Thanks, Sweta, for guiding us through the baby of the social channels!

Key areas we will cover in chapter 8:

✓ why B2B businesses are using Snapchat

✓ growing your Snapchat audience

✓ Snapchat strategies for your B2B organisation

✓ Snapchat perks for B2B businesses

✓ measuring the effectiveness of your Snapchat channel.

Snapchat is the youngest of all the sites mentioned in this book. It was officially released in 2011 and by November 2012, users had sent over one billion photos, making Snapchat as mainstream as the others and just as powerful.

Quick facts on Snapchat

Here are some interesting Snapchat facts:

▶ Five hundred million Snapchat stories are produced per day. It would take 158 years to watch all the stories.

▶ Sixty per cent of all smartphone users are on Snapchat.

▶ Snapchat has more users than Twitter.

▶ Snapchat has a higher video view rate than Facebook (Facebook: eight million views per day; Snapchat: 10 million views per day).

Why are B2B businesses using Snapchat?

The line that separates casual online social interactions from professional outreach efforts is becoming increasingly blurry for B2B marketers. While you've probably warmed up to promoting creatively through channels such as Facebook, YouTube and maybe even Pinterest, surely you must draw the line before a millennial selfie app such as Snapchat, right?

Wrong.

Let's take a step back and look at the current social media landscape. We have the top-five social networks: Facebook, Twitter, LinkedIn, YouTube and Pinterest. LinkedIn still holds the top rankings for B2B businesses. Yet, the unfortunate truth about these social networks is that, while they have millions of users, *their organic reach is getting smaller by the day.*

The reality is that to be seen on these social networks, you must advertise. Bids are getting more competitive and native ads are receiving fewer clicks. Long story short: social ad prices are rising while their results and effectiveness are falling.

Why Snapchat works

In the world of information overload, it's becoming fairly obvious why some ad types work and others don't. For example, webinar ads are not as effective as instant download ads. Why? Audiences are bombarded with information on a daily basis. The decision makers you are trying to reach barely have time to get lunch. What makes you think they have time to watch a webinar? On the other hand, instant downloads work well because prospects can download and apply them quickly.

So Snapchat is an attractive and viable channel for direct communication and relationship building. It's new, it's not overloaded and it happens to be a fantastic solution to the current challenges facing B2B marketers. It has over 150 million users and is constantly growing. That is why brands are increasingly considering Snapchat in their marketing mix. This chapter provides the metrics that matter for developing an effective strategy.

Using Snapchat for B2B

You can use Snapchat to easily communicate with people and receive a direct response without getting lost in their newsfeed. You may still be thinking, 'Well, the logic makes sense, but how can I get connected with my audience on Snapchat?'

The easiest way to promote your Snapchat channel is through the 'snapcode'. You can use your custom snapcode as an avatar on your social channels, which will allow your audience to quickly scan and add you. Snapchat has made QR codes cool again. You can also promote it on your email signature, through giveaways, at events and more.

Growing your audience on Snapchat

There are many tried and true strategies for building an audience on Snapchat. Let's go through a few of them.

Snapchat directories

Snapchat directories are the easiest way to increase the discoverability of your channel. Simply add your channel to different directories and an interested audience can easily find you. You can easily find your audience this way as well.

Once you find your audience, start engaging with them and building a rapport with them.

List of directories

Check out these Snapchat directories, which can help accelerate the audience growth process and increase your organisation's discoverability:

- www.addmesnaps.com

- www.ghostcodes.com.

Activity 1

Create your account and add your channel to the directories.

Influencer marketing via Snapchat

Another prominent Snapchat audience growth strategy revolves around Snapchat influencers and partnering with them for cross-promotional activities. For example, if you are launching a new service or solution, contact a prominent Snapchat user and let them know that you'd like to promote your solution to their audience.

Make them an offer they can't refuse; be generous in the way of what they will get out of it. They may be able to work out a bargain if your audiences align. Otherwise they may charge a set fee. It is up to the influencer, their time and the magnitude of the ask.

Secret Snapchat growth hack

Utilise every single channel you can to grow your number of followers:

▶ *On your website.* Create a mobile pop-up with the deep link to your Snapchat account. A deep link is a hyperlink that goes to a page beyond the home page of the linked site, accessing relevant material more directly. Snapchat deep links are always www.snapchat.com/add/YOURUSERNAME. For example, my Snapchat deep link is www.snapchat.com/add/swetaspeaks. You can find the deep link in Snapchat by selecting 'settings', 'add friends', 'share username'.

▶ *On your social channels.* Post deep links regularly where it is permitted and periodically change profile pictures to QR codes.

▶ *Offline materials.* Post your Snapchat QR code on every piece of marketing material you can think of.

5 strategies to increase audience engagement

You can build loyalty through giveaways and promotions to your Snapchat audience. Use promo codes and discounts, and provide insider access to incentivise them. Here are five ideas to get you thinking about creative ways you can engage your Snapchat audience:

▶ *Scavenger hunt in real time.* One year I created a scavenger hunt using Snapchat. The participants had to send snaps of specialty items they found all over the city of San Francisco. Those who found all six specialty items were given two free tickets to the Warriors game (live at the time). When you reward your fans on Snapchat, you are giving them a reason to follow you.

▶ *Utilising UGC (user-generated content).* The second way to engage your fans is by involving them in your stories. Share their relevant stories and feature this UGC on your other channels, where you can conveniently link your audience right to your Snapchat.

▶ *Content submission.* Third, engage your super fans by giving them the ability to submit content that will be posted from your account. You are essentially allowing them to create stories on your behalf. (When using this method, make sure to include your logo and branding.)

▶ *Exclusive content.* Fourth, provide exclusive content. This is the type of content they can't find anywhere except on your Snapchat channel. You can strengthen your channel's effectiveness by creating content that builds. Use cliffhangers at the end of posts, and keep them waiting for the next snap in your exclusive 'series' of content!

▶ *Referral codes.* Last, use referral codes to generate buzz around your community. Referral codes allow your fans to spread the word about your channel in return for something worthwhile to them. For example, when they refer their friends over, they will be able to get $10 off your product.

Useful Snapchat perks for B2B businesses

The strategies above are great for engagement, but what about specific B2B uses? Well, once you build a following, you can reach them with information in a personal way that is not intrusive (versus a text message).

Most people do not like giving away their personal number to businesses. They are even more adamant about minimising junk texts and sales calls than they are about protecting their email inbox.

An easy, non-invasive way to sidestep this is by contacting them through their Snapchat handle. Here are several examples.

Webinar reminders

One of the most useful ways to use Snapchat is to send mobile webinar reminders. The current norm is for a business to send a notice via email, but these emails can get lost in space, or prospects just don't open them.

A quick snap can work effectively because the recipients will receive a notification on their phone, and everything is optimised for mobiles.

Event updates

Most B2B companies host, attend and/or sponsor large events. When it is time to reach out to their audiences directly without asking for a phone number, Snapchat is an excellent solution.

Use snaps to send personal reminders, get feedback during and after the event and more.

Midway through the conference you can even send a simple snap that asks, 'Hi! How are you enjoying the seminar?' This frames the situation and builds a relationship with your customers at the same time!

Humanising your brand

A few short years ago, it was protocol to address a business as an entity and not a person. Times have changed and the online space has become so interconnected with human relationships that marketing has had to evolve to keep up. The online success of a company now lies in its ability to build powerful, human-like connections and develop very personal relationships with its customers.

Photography, videography and digital media are very successful forms of marketing because they have the power to communicate in an emotional and human way. Unfortunately, these are expensive and your ability to use them for every action is limited.

For day-to-day communications in real time, Snapchat provides an easy solution for you to connect with your customers and prospects. For example, you can easily invite a prospect to lunch or even send them a 'special tip of the day'. When you do this, you become a part of their daily social world.

Customer service

One of the best business uses for Snapchat video is to answer questions in real time. With a quick response rate, video snaps are a major perk for your customers. Using this function will increase trust in your brand, foster an exclusive relationship and encourage overall loyalty.

How to measure the effectiveness of your B2B Snapchat channel

It's important to understand where to find Snapchat analytics and how to use that data to make smart choices for your Snapchat marketing.

What are the five metrics that matter on Snapchat?

#1 Total opens

The total number, or aggregate, of views across all of your Snapchat stories is called total opens. This metric helps you gauge the success of a two-part strategy: content and growth. If you aren't receiving as many views of your content as you'd like, it's time to take a deeper look at these two facets of your Snapchat marketing plan.

Pro tip

To track your opens and views, you can use a tool such as www.snaplytics.io.

Content strategy

If users don't find any value in your snap, they're unlikely to view the other snaps in your story. Are your snaps interesting, funny and/or useful? Be honest with yourself and get feedback from others. Every snap you post should deliver value or fulfil a need, whether it's eliciting a human emotion or delivering information.

One way to boost views is to harness the power of anticipation. Snaps are short forms of content, but they should reflect the basic pillars of storytelling. Each video or series needs a beginning, middle and end ... and your audience needs a reason to follow through to the end.

Similar principles apply to images, which should take viewers on a journey that encourages them to keep watching and ask, 'What's next?' Unless you work somewhere inherently fun (such as Disneyland), snapping about your daily work life may not entice those who are viewing.

Businesses with successful view rates tend to keep their snaps brief and their stories one to two minutes long. Creating snap videos any longer than that can reduce viewer engagement.

Growth strategy

We have already gone through some of the strategies for finding your following on Snapchat. However, it takes dedicated time and constant learning to build a true and solid Snapchat family.

Is someone on your team a whiz at growing social networks? Are you allowing this person time dedicated to focusing on growth? You can't afford to slack on this. No-one wants to spend hours creating fabulous, witty content that will never find an audience.

#2 Monitor average open rates

Your Snapchat open rate is the percentage of total estimated followers who have engaged with your story. It's comparable to engagement rates on other social networks.

This metric is closely tied to the number of opens. Hence, your growth strategy takes a front seat when it comes to your success.

Pro tip

Repurpose your snaps for other social channels. Create short, trailer-like content pieces from your stories and share them on your other networks. Encourage viewers to follow you on Snapchat, where they can get the rest of the story.

Of course, if you don't have a viable audience on your other channels, this tactic won't help you. This brings us back to your growth strategy: who is the main social growth strategist (aka growth hacker) on your marketing team? If you don't have one, get one. If you can't afford one, become one. If your goal is to see success with social metrics, you cannot afford to underestimate the importance of this role.

#3 Track average screenshots

'Screenshots' is the number of screenshots people have taken of your snaps. This metric tells you how relevant and useful your snaps are to your audience. When users take a screenshot of a snap, you can assume it had value to them.

If you want to generate more screenshots, it's important to plan your content ahead of time. Create an editorial calendar with narratives you can use throughout the year. The goal is to purposefully create valuable content that is screenshot-worthy.

A few examples are checklists, inspirational quotes, audience spotlights, and discount coupons. If you're B2B, provide snackable content and event updates that encourage your audience to screenshot the details.

Overall, the screenshots metric shows you how engaged your audience is. If people are simply viewing your snaps without taking screenshots, there's room to grow engagement.

#4 Observe completion rate

Completion rate is the percentage of followers who viewed an entire story, from the first snap to the last. It's comparable to retention rate on other social networks.

This metric measures the loyalty of your audience. Do they want to see the content you're posting? Or are they watching the first snap and then opting out? You can increase the completion rate by providing content that's series-driven. When you keep your story brief and provide cause for interaction, your audience is more likely to watch it all the way through.

Use text to add calls to action on your snaps and tell your audience what to do next.

One common mistake businesses make is creating stories that don't connect. Their snaps are from random moments without context. If you plan to take a bunch of one-off snaps, use a longer frequency between each snap. One-off Snapchat campaigns are usually a day apart. But this tactic isn't recommended, as frequency is another metric that affects overall performance.

To increase your completion rate, send a snap to your audience with the same snap included in the story. This way they'll know you've added a story. Most users have story notifications turned off, so pinging your audience with an update can help increase the completion rate.

#5 Analyse follower growth

'Follower growth by source' is the key metric to determine where your Snapchat followers are coming from. From there, you can adjust your strategy.

Most Snapchat users are acquired by username. Once you find out how *your* followers are adding you, you can optimise the source to make it even better. For example, if most of your audience adds you through a snapcode, keep dishing that out and putting more effort in to receive even more results.

When you add friends, make sure they're following you back. One way to check is through the snap score. To view a user's snap score, tap on their username. Their snapcode will pop up with an avatar image, username and score (the number of snaps they've sent). If you don't see their score, they haven't added you back. In that case, contact them to follow up so you know they're receiving your stories.

Conclusion of chapter 8

Snapchat has become more than a selfie app for millennials. Witty business-minded entrepreneurs have discovered how to use the app to reach their B2B audiences in a fresh and new fashion.

Get started with Snapchat and find out just how useful it is for connecting with your audience in a personal and impactful way.

CHAPTER 9
Online etiquette

Key areas we will cover in chapter 9:

✓ you are what you share

✓ you've connected—now what?

✓ keeping in touch with your connections

✓ applying your good manners.

It might seem a little obvious that you need to behave online as you would in person, but for some reason we sometimes see the two differently and so act differently. You've probably seen snarky comments from individuals or conversations going off on a tangent and wondered why. The truth is, we have no body language to go on so we have to make do with 'digital body language' and use the tools we have at our disposal.

Let's have a look at some of the things we can do to make sure we don't upset anyone.

You are what you share

Everything you post online stays there forever and is a direct reflection on you, so beware of posting things that you wouldn't want your mother to see! You don't have to write everything yourself, but at least be aware of the whole content of what you are posting if it is an article from another source, and always include the link to the original article. That way, the rightful owner of the content gets the attribution. Remember, 'you are what you share'.

Working with original content

So where will your content come from? Once you have started your social media plan from chapter 1, you should have a clear understanding of what your social media efforts are going to achieve for you.

Your content will come from:

▶ *personal content*: your own efforts from articles, videos and blog posts

▶ *third-party content*: respected industry online publications. The emphasis here is on respected, professional and interesting content.

When it comes to third-party content, it is important you don't simply copy the article onto your site and make it your own, as you could find yourself in trouble for a copyright breach. It is, however, perfectly acceptable to mention what the article is about and link back to the original article so that the original author gets the attribution.

Making connections with LinkedIn

Very few people ignore you in real-life, face-to-face networking situations, so why do they online? The simple answer is because they probably don't realise they are! There are many things we do online that we wouldn't dream of doing in person, so let's go through a few of them to make sure you stand out for being a pleasure to know online.

Think about whether you follow up every LinkedIn connection request you get. Many people simply click 'accept' and think no more of it. When someone requests to connect with you and you click 'accept' with no effort to carry on the conversation, you are basically saying 'hello' and ending the conversation there. All you gain by doing this is a string of connections that don't have any real value: you become a connection collector, which you wouldn't do when face-to-face networking as that would be rude.

So how can you use social etiquette to really make your LinkedIn connections valuable and to stand out from the crowd at the same time? I suggest you view LinkedIn as your own boardroom of connections versus your coffee-shop connections on Twitter or Facebook. Your connections on LinkedIn tend to be managers, directors, business owners, CEOs and the like, and could be a very different set of connections from those on your Facebook page.

Send personalised connection requests

When you first send a possible contact an invitation on LinkedIn, do it from their profile page by clicking the 'connect' button.

We will use Paul as an example. By adding Paul this way rather than just going to the 'add connections' tab, you can send a personalised message, such as, 'Thanks for the coffee yesterday. It was great to catch up'. This gives you the opportunity to remind Paul where you know him from, which is particularly useful if you're getting back in touch after a long period of time, such as with someone from an old job or your school days.

If you send a connection request from the 'add connections' box, there is no facility to personalise your message, so avoid this where possible. It might be a quick and easy way to add a handful of new connections, but it's much better to spend the time and do it right by adding your personal touch to each one individually.

Reply when accepting a connection request

All too often I receive the standard email from LinkedIn that says a connection request has been accepted, but I rarely get a short message from the new connection at least saying 'hi'.

When Paul has accepted my connection request, he could then send a short message back. I like to take a look at my new connection's profile if I am not too familiar with them, and find something I can comment on. Maybe he comes from my hometown, or works for a company I know well, or perhaps I can see from his interests that he too is a cyclist. Whatever it may be, try and find something to start a short conversation and build on your relationship together: make the effort to find out more, just as you would in person.

Activity 1

Go to your LinkedIn page and search for connections you admire within your industry. Are you able to connect with them? Are they in a group with you?

I've covered a couple of the initial and basic steps we tend to forget about, so now let's look at composing a message to a group of connections on LinkedIn.

Keep in touch with your connections

You can send a message to only 50 people at a time and this is a good thing—otherwise I am sure you would see a lot of spam—but there are a couple of things to note here.

If you're sending an email to a group of connections, think about your greeting. How are you going to address them? I suggest you start with something like 'Hi everyone' or 'Greetings to you all' and then immediately say 'Please excuse my lack of personalisation in this email as I am sending this out to a group of connections'. That way, you can be forgiven and you have addressed any possible bad-manners critics. Or personalise them by creating the messages one at a time. Unfortunately, you can't hide the names of everyone within the 'conversation', though actual email addresses are not visible.

Consider your message content

If you want your connections to leave you in droves, then feel free to write about all the good things you do or your company offers! I have made this mistake in the past myself until I came to my senses. I realised I needed to treat this form of communication the same way as my newsletters — that is, by adding valuable resources. People don't want to hear about you and what you can offer all the time, but they do want to know how you may be able to help fix their problems.

One example of a message to my connections looked like figure 9.1.

Figure 9.1: example email to connections

Hi everyone,

Please excuse the lack of personalisation in this message as it is coming to you through LinkedIn.

I wanted to let you all in on three pieces of information that may be of use to your business in the very near future.

The first thing I wanted to share is a book I am reading called *Contagious: Why Things Catch On* by Jonah Berger. It is a superb, easy-to-read book, packed full of things to help with your social marketing. One to keep hold of and refer back to time and again.

You may also be interested to know that xxx and xxx have partnered together for an event and that Richard Branson will perform a free 45-minute webinar this Wednesday at 1 pm. If you are interested, I have attached the registration link below. Please also feel free to pass it on to any other contacts you feel may benefit.

Here is the link: www.xxxxxxxx.xx.

Finally, this company is giving some of the large stationery retailers a run for their money with pricing. Take a look at xxxxxxxxxxxxxxxx.

That's about it for passing on a bit of information. I hope you find some, if not all of it, of use.

Kind regards,
Linda, Blue Banana

There was nothing in the message about my company—only three bits of information I thought would be great to pass on. It contained a reference to a great book that most businesses could probably utilise, a free event being put on by two companies and a website that may save a business a bit of money.

By keeping in touch this way, my aim is to add value but, at the same time, to put myself back on the radar of my connections.

Activity 2

Create your own message to send out to your connections, taking care not to make it all about you.

Ask for recommendations

Recommendations are a valuable part of your LinkedIn profile and could be the one thing that gets you the deal when a possible client is assessing you against your competitor. Most people only have a couple of recommendations, so you can stand out from the crowd by having a large number of genuine and applicable ones. A good number to aim for is 10.

You will notice that the recommendation request form is another auto-generated template, so it needs personalising: you will need to personalise both the body of the message and the subject line. I like to change mine to read something like 'Recommendation request' as the subject line and 'Are you able to write a recommendation about the presentation I did for your company last week?' in the main body. Don't make the request too long, but be clear on what you want a recommendation for.

If you are asking Paul for a recommendation about a seminar he attended that you spoke at, you could change the message to say, 'I hope you enjoyed the seminar last week. If you feel that you are able to write a brief recommendation about how you found my presentation and speaking skills, I would appreciate it. I totally understand if you would prefer not to. Kind regards ...'

There is no need to open your message with 'Dear ...', as LinkedIn will automatically add that in for you — just choose your greeting from the drop-down box.

In a nutshell, you should look at personalising every aspect of LinkedIn that you can, making each and every standard template your own. It may take you a little longer, but the value you'll get from doing the job right will far outweigh the effort.

Ask yourself, if you were meeting face to face, what would you be doing differently? People easily judge on first impressions, so make yours a great one each and every time you connect.

> **Activity 3**
>
> Ask for five recommendations to add to your profile.

Applying good manners online

So what about etiquette for the other sites, including Facebook? I asked fellow speaker, author and trainer Kevin Knebl what he thinks about social media etiquette for both business and pleasure. Kevin spends his days educating companies big and small on the benefits of using social media and being social to one another. This is what he said.

> Facebook is the world's largest high school reunion. When I graduated from high school in 1982, back when the Earth was cooling, I had a little black book that contained my girlfriend's phone number and the phone numbers of some of my drinking buddies. Facebook isn't a mood ring, pet rock or hula hoop. It's been here a long time with no sign of leaving: it's growing every day.

Communication platforms are always changing. I'm sure that the telephone was a real shocker for the smoke signal and two cans and a string set. Facebook is just one of the current state-of-the-art tools in terms of communication platforms. And that's an important point: it's a communication channel. In a more and more interconnected, over-caffeinated, hyper-competitive, 24/7/365 world, Facebook is a great way to stay in touch with huge numbers of people, take the pulse of society and generally keep in contact with the world.

The paradox is that while we're all connecting online, there is not a lot different about our communication styles. I often have people ask me after my speaking engagements, 'How should I be online?' My answer is usually, 'Well, unless you have a multiple-personality disorder, you should be pretty much the way you are offline'. No matter where you go, there you are.

All things being equal, people do business with and refer business to people they know, like and trust. By this point in the twenty-first century most of us have gotten past the Madison Avenue slick come-on lines we're constantly fed. I don't know about you, but I'm looking for authenticity, transparency and honesty. Save the slickness. Just tell me the truth. I can make an intelligent buying decision based on truth and appreciation for the consumer. The smart businesses know this and treat their customers with respect.

On the social side of social networking, when someone sends you a 'friend request' on Facebook, you can click on their name and check out their profile before you accept their request. This is probably a smart move. You wouldn't just accept someone's request to connect by mail or phone without knowing who you are connecting with, would you? The same goes for social networking. Only now you can learn about someone far more thoroughly than you could prior to social networking. Whatever you post on your Facebook wall and other online profiles is pretty much public information depending on your privacy settings. You now have the ability to see what someone is posting on their Facebook wall (to a degree), which groups they are a member of, who their friends are and much more information, which gives you some insight into who they are. By extension, this allows you to determine who you are connecting with, with far greater accuracy than in the past.

But no matter how sophisticated you are at social networking, it will never be a replacement for good social skills. And this is huge. Most people figure out what they want to do for a living and forget that unless they are Tom Hanks living on a deserted island with a volleyball named Wilson, people skills are a critical piece of their success puzzle. And herein lies a huge paradox. No matter how many connections you have on social networking platforms, it's all about relationships. You don't have a relationship with your computer; you have a relationship 'through' your computer. So no matter how sophisticated technology gets, we still build true relationships the old-fashioned way — by taking a sincere interest in people.

The sophisticated person understands that huge doors of opportunity swing on little hinges. When we take a sincere interest in other people, we can build relationships — real relationships, not just a connection. You can 'connect' with the whole world but if you don't really connect, you may as well be looking at a worldwide phonebook.

Emojis

While they may seem a little childish on the surface, smiley, angry and other emotion icons are a great way to show the tone you are trying to get across in a comment. For example, how would you read this comment:

I don't know how you have the time to write such posts.

You could take that comment one of two ways. Either they are having a dig at you because you should be doing something more productive, or they are in awe that you have the time to write such posts. If you don't know the person, you have no context for how they mean it and could quite easily be upset by it and shoot back a reply that is over the top, sending the individual into a spin. However, if they added a smiley emoji to their comment, you would instantly know the spirit in which the comment was intended. Emojis can save an awful lot of headaches!

Conclusion of chapter 9

Remember to be yourself online and then you won't forget your natural online manners either.

If you are well known for supplying great information, it will go a long way to establishing your online brand, so it's important to keep up the great content part of your plan. Use a good proportion of your own material, but no more than, say, about 30 per cent: you don't want to be seen as a spammer.

CHAPTER 10
Email marketing

I asked Glenn Edley, Tez and the team at Spike to write this chapter on email marketing because that's all they do all day—email marketing. We may as well learn from the masters! Below, you'll find the answers to many of your email marketing questions as well as lots more that you didn't know you didn't know about.

Key areas we will cover in chapter 10:

✓ using email marketing

✓ building a list

✓ designing your email

✓ making sure it's working

✓ allowing for mobile phone use.

Effective email marketing will unlock the value from your prospects and customers and build a solid foundation on which you can build a successful marketing campaign.

Quick facts on email marketing

Here are some interesting email marketing facts:

▶ Fifty-three per cent of email readers open on mobile.

▶ About 2.5 billion people have smartphones.

▶ Remote workers don't always use a computer.

What is email marketing?

Email marketing is sending your message directly to a relevant consumer's inbox. It's delivered; they don't *need* to go anywhere to find it. Think about it: an email can be in your hand on your phone, it's often personalised and it's usually tailored to particular tastes and preferences. What other medium can do that? Every other method of marketing, such as magazines or billboards, sends out a message to a huge audience in the hope people respond. It might work, it might not, but an *email* can get right in front of relevant eyeballs if done correctly.

Apart from direct cold telephone calling, there is no more direct method of communication in the marketing sphere.

Best return on investment

With traditional forms of advertising, it's hard to fathom where your money has gone. Maybe you've generated brand awareness; maybe you've generated a customer. In reality, it's nigh on impossible to tell, or measure.

Things are different with email marketing.

Every email sent creates data. This data can show how long someone spent looking at the content, whether they clicked any links and which links they clicked. With more specialist software and a deeper look, you can see if they made a purchase and even how much they spent. This enables you to see which promotions/

products are working well, those that aren't working so well, and which customers are more likely to click through than others.

With this data, you'll see the exact ROI on dollar-spent to dollar-earned and can make marketing decisions based on concrete sales data.

Getting started

Before starting any new campaign it's important to think about the following:

▶ *Audience.* What demographic of people are on your database? You need to speak their language and create offers that are relevant to them.

▶ *Targeted vs non-targeted.* Is this email going to the whole database or to a specific segment where you can target the message to them?

▶ *Message.* What is the one thing you want people to take away from your email?

▶ *Goal.* This is your purpose or what you want to achieve. Is it brand awareness, sales, feedback or to impart information? If you try to combine everything all at once you may give people too many choices so they end up choosing nothing.

▶ *Design.* Do you have a look and feel/design in mind? Are there brand guidelines to follow? Should the emails match the website?

Answer these questions ahead of time and you'll have a much clearer and more effective email marketing plan. It will also ensure you match your business objectives and send only email with purpose.

Build a list

Collect, curate, continue.

A 'list' is your spreadsheet of customers/clients and their contact details. If you're meticulous and savvy about your records you can divide this list up into smaller lists based on buying habits, location, age, gender, hobbies and so on—in fact, anything you can think of that will allow better targeting and a stronger message to reach your audience.

A good list will contain:

▶ first and last name

▶ email address

▶ location.

Keep this database on your computer and also on a secure server, preferably backed up in the cloud.

Give people a reason to sign up to your emails. For example, if someone purchases for the first time, they could be offered 10 per cent on their *next* purchase if they sign up to your newsletter, or you could run a contest offering a prize where entry is via email, or you could give an ebook away in exchange for their details.

After sending a few emails, you'll notice trends appearing. If certain people buy certain products more often than others it's possible (and recommended) to tailor the content of their future emails to their interests. Do they like books in a certain genre, or music from a certain artist? The data collected can be put to use in your marketing initiatives such as running a promotion on relevant products or helping you further divide your list.

Activity 1

Start creating your list with your current customers' details.

Design

Some points to keep in mind:

▶ *Tone.* Think about the tone of your copy: does it match your business?

▶ *Look and feel.* Think about the look and feel: does it match your brand?

When creating the layout for your email it's important to consider the following:

▶ *Design for email.* A printed flyer may not necessarily work in email form.

▶ *Navigation.* How easy is it for people to get through your email? Especially with longer emails it's important to be able to scan quickly for content that is of particular interest.

▶ *Length of email.* Would your email be more effective broken down into smaller pieces and sent over a few days? If it's too long, then content at the bottom could be missed.

▶ *Plain text email.* A plain text email is just that — plain text. No images, no HTML, no hyperlinks, just text. Plain text can be useful as some devices (smart watches) only display text, spam filters don't flag plain text emails, some email clients don't handle HTML very well and some readers might just prefer it.

▶ *100 KB limit.* In Gmail an email stops loading when it gets to 100 KB, so you'll see the message, 'This message is only partially downloaded. Download remaining 6.6 KB'. Not ideal. A shorter email will have less HTML code, so there's less chance it will get this message. For longer emails there is a chance the customer won't click to download the remaining code and never see the bottom of your email.

▶ *Maximum width 600 px.* This ensures your email looks its best across different screen sizes and email clients.

Quick tip

To make the email less likely to be treated as spam, also create a plain text version.

Top of the email

The subject line and preheader are the first things your audience will read, and they play a pivotal role in getting people to open your emails.

▶ *Subject line.* This needs to be enticing and clear. Subject line length is less important as modern devices display the whole line.

▶ *Preheader.* This is a valuable piece of content that is often overlooked. Use this content to build on the subject line. In Gmail, Outlook and on iPhone this text displays under the subject line as preview text (usually around one hundred characters).

▶ *Personalised 'From' address.* People are more likely to open an email from an actual person; for example, Kelly@ rather than info@.

▶ *Link to view/read online.* This is not necessary if an email is fully tested across all popular email programs.

▶ *Link to subscribe.* A handy addition. This way, if your email is forwarded, the recipient has an easy way of joining your list.

Quick tip

Wherever possible, do not have 'Trouble viewing this email ...', 'Read online' or 'Unsubscribe' displaying in the teaser text.

Content

For the main body of your email, there are some guidelines to follow that will make it more effective:

▶ *Clear calls to action.* Think about what you want the customer to do. If they need to take action, make it obvious; for example, insert an instruction to 'Click here!'

▶ *Use short sentences and paragraphs.* You want your customer to keep reading, not fall asleep.

▶ *Use white space* to make it easy to read and draw your eye to different content.

▶ *Add hyperlinks.* Link your articles/products/images back to your website for more information and an easy purchase.

▶ *Use text formatting* such as bold text, bullet points and subheadings for effect.

▶ *Use spacing and horizontal lines* to separate content areas.

▶ *Use web-safe fonts only.* Alternatively, you can use images to display text in a different font, but only use these where necessary as they add size to your email.

▶ *Use social sharing and 'Forward to a friend' links* to increase open rates and grow your database.

Quick tip

These are our suggested minimum font sizes:

■ body text: 14 pt

■ header text: 22 pt.

Remember, in today's mobile-first world your email will be read on a small screen.

Above all, keep the content relevant to your audience. By dealing with their problems and offering them a solution in line with your content plan, you should never be at a loss for what to write each month.

Images

Images speak louder than words, so use them to emphasise your message. There are some important points to note:

▶ *Alternative text*. Always use alternative (alt) text for images. By combining these with styles and background colours you can create an attractive 'images off' email where your message is still visible. 'Alt text' is words or phrases used in HTML to tell the website viewers the content of an image. Alt text appears in a blank box that would normally contain the image and can be incredibly useful when an image link is not available or when an image is not supported in the recipient's email program.

▶ *Background images*. These aren't supported in all email clients so ensure the email is still 'attractive' without them.

▶ *Image size*. Always resize and optimise your images with Photoshop or a similar app. Do not exceed the maximum width of the email and scale images to 72 dpi (dots per inch). The smaller in file size your images are, the quicker your email will load. Photoshop has a 'save for web' function, which removes all the unnecessary data from image files.

▶ *Animated GIFs*. These are okay in moderation and can add great visual impact to an otherwise static email.

▶ *Image-to-text ratio*. Too much text is off-putting. Too many images might get the email flagged as spam and not seen. Strike a healthy balance between images and words. Bear in mind that on average 24 per cent of email text is read thoroughly, but 80 per cent of images are seen.

▶ *Images-only emails*: Although images-only emails are sometimes necessary, we suggest keeping the preheader and footer as text elements, otherwise the email could be flagged as spam.

Footer

The footer of an email usually includes contact details, social links and other general information about the company. Some notes:

▶ *Why me?* It's good practice to include, 'You are receiving this email because you signed up on our website' or a similar message to remind people of why they're receiving the email. This will cut down on spam complaints lodged against the sender's email address.

▶ *What are spam complaints?* This is when someone clicks the 'Mark as spam' or 'Report as junk' button in an email. Some people also use this as a lazy way to unsubscribe so remember to include an unsubscribe link.

▶ *Unsubscribe link.* It is a legal requirement to include this: even the most loyal customer may want to break up the relationship some time. The 'unsubscribe' link has to be clear and must be a one-click unsubscribe rather than the 'send an email to this address with unsubscribe in the subject line ...' method. When contacting an old or inactive list, consider adding an extra unsubscribe link in the header. Don't worry about unsubscribes — you want a clean list with only those on it who want to hear from you.

Quick tip

It's good practice to include your company name, address and contact details — it just adds to your credibility.

Designing for mobile phones

A huge 53 per cent of email readers opened their email on a portable device in 2016.

Creating a mobile-friendly version is crucial as the number of people opening email on mobile phones increases. It's the new norm. Think about the following:

▶ *Optimised for mobile.* If you aren't using responsive code—that is, when it automatically fits the screen in a way that's easy to read—ensure your email is still readable on a small screen.

▶ *Calls to action.* These must be tappable on a touchscreen with image sizes a minimum of 44 × 44 pixels.

▶ *Layout.* Increase font sizes, line heights and the use of white space to make the layout finger-navigation friendly.

▶ *One-column format works best for mobile.* Anything else becomes hard to read.

Testing

Test! Test! Test! Then test again.

Once the email has been built, it is important to test the hell out of it, ensuring the customer will see it the way it was intended. Test your HTML code across all major email clients to ensure your email displays correctly for all your customers. If an email is broken, you could lose that customer. Litmus and Email on Acid are great, simple, easy-to-use programs for ensuring email readability across all clients and platforms.

Proofread your content and get it peer reviewed before sending in case you have missed something. Typoes an Bad Grama doesnt look good!

Your database is invaluable so spending a few minutes to triple check everything is worth it.

> **Quick tip**
>
> Adding the Litmus tracking code will help you to identify your database's specific viewing habits.

Database

A lot goes on behind the scenes besides simply building the email. Maintaining your database is incredibly important. Regularly sending emails to your list helps keep the database fresh and engaged with your content.

We suggest sending emails at least monthly and sticking to a schedule. This will help create user habits so your customers will come to expect your email. For infrequent sends to less active lists there is a risk of people marking you as spam simply because they forgot they even signed up.

When trying to grow your database, use these ideas to get started:

▶ *Collect contacts in-store and online.* Run competitions where entry is via email; if you have an event, take a signup form.

▶ *Use competitions and tell-a-friend promotions.*

▶ *Collect more data from customers to enable targeted emails.* For example, add new fields to the signup forms, then create content-specific campaigns to the users' interests or demographic.

> **Quick tip**
>
> If people aren't opening your monthly emails, target these people with a re-engagement campaign to get them back on board.

Sending

When should you send your emails, and should you resend them?

We normally schedule emails anywhere between 10 am and 3 pm, but there are no hard rules around this—it is really dependent on your database.

Collect information on when emails are opened. It's a good idea to try sending at different times, or sending the same email at different times to different lists in order to get some concrete data on the best open times.

Resending emails to those contacts who haven't opened your latest email is a great way to encourage more readers. We suggest changing the subject line and preheader text on these resends.

Be aware of your audience. International emails need to be relevant, double checked for spelling (optimize vs optimise) and sent at appropriate times.

Quick tip

Resends win! After sending an email, wait two to three days and then resend to the people who *didn't* open the first time around.

Activity 2

Choose your email marketing campaign provider. MailChimp is extremely popular, as are Constant Contact, Aweber and Infusionsoft.

Lifecycle emails

Lifecycle emails are automated messages sent to a (usually inactive) contact after a certain period of time (such as one month, two months, or six months, for example). These emails are used to remind the recipient to take action (activate a card, pop in for an oil change or save 10 per cent, for example) and convert them into active customers, usually by offering them a reason to get back on track and involved with your business.

As lifecycle emails are usually automated they're a great way to get in touch and reconnect with those customers who may have slipped through the cracks. If there is no contact from the recipient after 12 months they are typically removed from the database.

Conclusion of chapter 10

This might sound like a lot of work and time, but once your database is up and running it's a matter of maintenance. Think of your database like a garden: the ground needs to be cleared, then you add your plants, then once the hard work is done all that's required is a little pruning here, some feeding and watering, and a bit of attention to allow it to flourish.

CHAPTER 11

Podcasting

Key areas we will cover in chapter 11:

✓ choosing a topic

✓ how to go about podcasting

✓ some real-life experiences.

While we have looked at the most common social media platforms, there are also many others. Personally, I don't have time to 'trial' them all. Instead, I wait until others have done that and then I decide if it's worth my time to use them; you may do the same. As the saying goes, it's the *second* mouse that gets the cheese!

Quick facts on podcasting

Here are some interesting podcasting facts:

▶ Sixty-four per cent of podcasts are listened to on a smartphone or tablet.

▶ Podcast listeners consume five shows per week on average.

▶ Twenty-one per cent of Americans over the age of 12 listened to a podcast in the past month.

▶ There are over one billion subscribers on iTunes alone.

What is a podcast?

Think of a podcast as a short radio show on a particular subject that interests you and is delivered to your smartphone and out through your headset or player.

Do you listen to the radio or do you spend your travel time listening to podcasts like many people do, particularly if you are on a bus or train? It's not just music or audiobooks going on in people's headphones. Podcasts are now huge and there is one on just about every subject you can think of. I listen to several each week, and I *really* look forward to the next episode of my favourites landing on my phone. In fact, going back to the radio when I don't have a podcast to listen to seems strange now. And they don't all need to be about work. My husband subscribes to several cycling podcasts because that is his hobby and learning more or listening to interviews educates and motivates. One of my hobbies is writing fiction so I listen to podcasts on writing and publishing as well as marketing. I can use the marketing knowledge podcasts for both business and pleasure because there is always something to learn.

Don't be scared!

The first time I ever recorded an audio and put it out there I was worried I'd do something wrong, say the wrong thing or annoy people, but once I got over myself and realised it didn't have to be perfect, it was plain sailing. Remember, to launch something, it doesn't have to be perfect — it just needs to work. Think about how many updates Microsoft has done in its time—it didn't launch a perfect product right at the beginning and even now it adds updates and fixes bugs. Your podcasts, in fact everything you do marketing wise, will get better as you go.

Activity 1

What interests you that you could start a podcast on? Write a list. It could be business-related or hobby-related.

Getting started

Some people prefer to make podcasts rather than videos because they are not on camera, just on microphone. Just like the chapter on video, there is some basic equipment you'll need, but you can make a start with your smartphone and the basic audio editing software you may have on your computer, such as GarageBand. My very first one was an audio version of an article I had published on LinkedIn, the idea being that those who were time poor could listen to the article rather than read it. Whatever your reason for giving it a go, you'll need somewhere to host the files and some means of getting the podcasts to your audience. I'll share what I have done because I like it easy.

Get the recording

Your smartphone audio recorder is a good starting place, though a professional microphone would be much better if you have the budget. Google what others are using and make your own decision according to your budget. Make sure there is no background noise and make a clear recording of what you want to say; then save the file. I save it to Dropbox directly from my phone and then access it from there. If you can do it without the need for editing, all the better and easier it will be for you — in fact, many podcasts don't get edited because it makes them more natural. If you are interviewing someone who is not in the same room as you, you can Skype them and record the conversation. There are various software options available, depending on your computer, to make this a bit easier and give you the best recording results. Either way, you end up with an audio file ready work with.

Top and tail it

You'll need to pre-record an introduction—which is usually a couple of minutes—about what is on your show this episode, as well as an ending or outro. The latter usually thanks the listener for tuning in and promotes the business a little—a neat way to wrap everything up. These two sections are then added onto the main audio file via your audio editing software to create one file.

Upload and share

Take a look at www.soundcloud.com and www.podbean.com. Both are free or have a paid version for more functionality. It's as simple as uploading your file to the site and making it available for others to listen to. If you use PodBean, you can link that to the iTunes store for easy subscription and access—the easier you can make it for your listeners, the better. If you use SoundCloud, you will need to point people to your channel, or you can embed the file into your website or blog post. Just like YouTube, there's basic information to fill in when you've uploaded your podcast and also a space to add the written content version or transcript of the content if you have it—great for the search engines.

Activity 2

Create your account at PodBean and upload your first recording so you understand the process.

Podcasts are another great way to get your thoughts and ideas, or publicise others' knowledge, via interviews and to promote your own brand at the same time. Interviewing other thought leaders and sharing that knowledge is also great for your own learning and networking. Who wouldn't want to record an interview with someone they admire?

Activity 3

Link your PodBean channel to iTunes ready for your first proper podcast!

I asked Craig Oliver of The Project Guys about his experiences creating and delivering podcasts. His show is called 'Talking Better Business' and he was happy to share his story.

Real story: Talking Better Business

Craig started because he wanted to reach more people with his message and develop content for his social sites at the same time. He hated writing and knew that articles would never get written if it was down to him. That, coupled with his passion of talking to others and learning, made podcasting the obvious choice.

Talk about what?

As Craig coaches SMEs, a podcast interviewing clients and other business owners about their successes and failures was the most obvious topic. It would not only give his listeners, but also himself, valuable information and learnings. He started with his low-hanging fruit—his clients—then progressed out to his wider network. Getting guests on the show has never been a problem and he allows them—in fact, he encourages them—to share the podcast they've created with their network for greater exposure and thought leadership all round.

(continued)

Real story: Talking Better Business *(cont'd)*

How often should you podcast?

Craig originally thought he would create one podcast per month, but his own coach advised him that in order to get traction, he needed to do it weekly as monthly was a 'long time between drinks'. It may seem an awful lot to commit to but Craig feels it's worth it and has committed to creating 40 per year. The key here is to be organised. Craig always has around seven podcasts in the bag created and ready to roll, and in fact didn't officially launch until he had seven in the can.

What about equipment?

For the very first ones, Craig used his smartphone internal microphone but he very quickly wanted to create a better experience so he did some research and found recording tools to suit his experience and budget.

When it comes to editing, he likes to leave the recording fairly raw and in fact tells the audience it's a 'warts and all' interview, keeping it real. If there is any real editing to be done, he gives it to his virtual assistant (VA) to do. In fact, it was his VA that found the right equipment as well as the app for creating the intro and outro. Or you could Google and use a paid service to create one for you for under $200.

What has it given you?

More and more people have heard about Craig and The Project People so he has gained notoriety in the business space. He also gets his VA to write up an article from the audio file, which he posts, giving him SEO benefits and, of course, another piece of content to use elsewhere. In another couple of years, he knows he'll be well ahead in the game, having built a back catalogue and audience while others are still thinking about getting going.

His advice to get going with podcasting?

'Imperfect action is better than perfect inaction. Just get on and have a go because even if you stuff it up, your audience in the beginning will be small and you have to start somewhere. Microsoft never sends a perfect product out—that's why there are continual updates.'

You can find the shows at www.talkingbetterbusiness.com. Think about the topic you'd like to talk about and make a start—before your competitors do.

This is Katie's story; she believes you need to find your niche to stand out.

Real story: Empire by Design

I started a podcast in 2014 when it was still a relatively unknown/ un-embraced platform beyond the really early adopters. At the time, I was one of only two podcasts globally interviewing wellness entrepreneurs/business owners about their business and marketing. My podcast—Empire by Design—has become an exploration of empire-building journeys, including personal branding, mindset and podcasting interviews with female entrepreneurs.

Having a podcast has allowed me to build influence and authority in my niche very quickly. It's enabled me to connect with influencers and brought me some of my most high-value clients. I began teaching other entrepreneurs to podcast in 2015 and it has been extremely rewarding to see the impact podcasting has on someone's mindset and presence around their business.

(continued)

> ### Real story: Empire by Design *(cont'd)*
>
> In 2017, I think podcasting is becoming a more crowded market so it's important for people to niche down in order to stand out from the crowd. My podcast is experimenting a lot more with solo shows (rather than the popular interview-based show) and on-air coaching calls, which are an excellent way for people to experience working with me first hand.

Conclusion of chapter 11

Content can come in many forms and indeed a piece of content can be changed into another form. From a blog post can come a podcast; from a customer question can come a blog post—and it goes on. What content do you have already that you can practise podcasting with?

CHAPTER 12
Google+

Key areas we will cover in chapter 12:

✓ the advantages of Google+

✓ deciding if Google+ is for you

✓ creating a Google+ page

✓ Google+ functions.

Google+ is a social media platform that sits somewhere between Facebook and LinkedIn. Owned by Google, it has great search engine capabilities, particularly for a bricks-and-mortar business. I debated whether to add this chapter in since the platform has not been a huge success for Google, but it does have some benefits for you, so let's explore it.

Quick facts on Google+

Here are some interesting Google+ facts:

▶ It was launched in 2011.

▶ There are over 2.5 billion registered users worldwide but 90 per cent are thought to have never used it.

▶ It once stipulated that if you wanted any other Google product, such as Gmail, you had to open a Google+ account too, which is one reason it has created such a large user base.

Advantages of Google+

With Facebook being your coffee shop of conversation, and LinkedIn being your boardroom, it's hard to see where Google+ fits in—and that has meant its growth and active user base has been slow to catch on.

It's just like when a new bar opens up in your town. Until your mates start hanging out there, you stick with the existing haunts, and it's exactly the same in the online space. If your buddies are happily using Facebook, you will too—there is little point in going to a bar on your own.

However, there are some definite advantages to having a Google+ page, and Google has thought very hard about how it can bring some unique functionality to the platform. Here are some of the advantages:

▶ *The search engine optimisation (SEO) aspect.* Obviously, Google owns the Google+ accounts, just as it owns YouTube, so when it comes to popping up high on search results, it's going to favour its own content from its own members over and above another platform or website.

▶ *The ability to hold a Google+ Hangout.* This is basically a live video chat, similar to Skype, where you can invite a group of people into the conversation. The quality is great and it's easy to use—and a great way to demonstrate your product or offer help to a group of people free of charge.

▶ *You can put those you follow into 'circles'.* Think of a circle as a folder: groups of people such as friends, acquaintances, heroes, business connections and so on, that you can name whatever you like. When you post an update, the 'public' option will come up. You then have the option to send that post to certain circles. There is no limit to the number of circles you can have.

The rest of the functionality of Google+ is pretty much the same as Facebook and LinkedIn, with the ability to:

► post content

► share content

► comment on content

► like (+1)

► send messages

► create events

► include links

► add video

► add photos

► use hashtags

► use @replies

► build a following (circle).

Who should have a Google+ page?

So who should use Google+? Is it for every business? I would say if you are a bricks-and-mortar business, the answer to that is a resounding *yes*, if only for the SEO benefits. It's also a really important tool for a business that might not otherwise bother with a website, such as a local fish and chip shop or corner grocery store. Think about how you yourself use Google's search function. If you were new to the area, maybe even visiting on holiday, you would probably put 'fish and chips' and the town you are in into the search box and hit 'enter' from your smartphone. If there is a Google+ page, or even a Google My Business page (more on that in chapter 13), it will come up in the listing, along with a map showing the location. There might also be opening hours, telephone number and physical address details, so all in all it's very handy. The fact that the service is free is a great incentive for any business, no matter how small, to get started and gain some online presence. Add to that the customer reviews that the local fish and chip shop could get from visitors to the page and it's a no-brainer.

Some Google+ ideas

There are many examples of brands that use Google+ well. Take a look at the following ones to get inspiration about how you can use it for your business:

- plus.google.com/+starbucks

- plus.google.com/+wholefoods

- plus.google.com/+Nordstrom

- plus.google.com/+marksandspencer.

Creating a Google+ page

It's easy to get started: simply go to www.accounts.google.com and create a Google account, if you don't already have one, then follow the steps to creating a Google+ page.

Activity 1

Set up your Google+ page and copy some of the content from your Facebook page across so it doesn't look empty. It has now become part of your digital marketing strategy and needs updating regularly.

You can and should have more than one admin or page manager — Google actually allows you to have up to 50 at any one time. Only the page owner can add or remove page managers, although page managers can remove themselves.

Adding a manager

To add another manager to your Google+ page, click 'settings' and look for your account. Click 'manage permissions' to enter their email address or invite them by their profile — then you just need to click 'invite'.

This page displays all of the active managers, as well as anyone you have just invited to become a manager. When the manager invitation has been accepted, the owner of the Google+ page will be notified via email. It's worth pointing out that the page owner and all of the managers can view the names and email addresses of the other managers listed on this page.

Removing a manager

To remove a manager, or to remove yourself as a manager of a page, simply click the 'x' associated with the person you'd like to remove.

When a manager is removed, both the former manager and the page owner will be notified and advised who removed them. This is a great bit of security, particularly if you have a large team looking after the page.

Transferring ownership of a page

If you are unsure about who the page owner should be — the business owner or the marketing department, for instance — or if someone leaves the company, you can always transfer ownership if necessary later on. The person you transfer ownership to must have been an existing manager of the page for at least two weeks. If you don't have any managers, you need to first invite someone to become a manager and then wait for them to accept the invitation. When an owner transfers ownership to someone else, the old owner automatically becomes a manager of the page and the transfer of ownership happens immediately—no confirmation is necessary from the new owner. It's worth noting that switching ownership of the page does not switch the ownership of other Google services linked to your page. Just make sure you are using Google+ as the relevant page before you add or remove anyone.

The internal pages

Let's look at the basic page functionality. Like the other platforms, Google changes things and adds things with the wind, but the basics will usually stay the same.

Home page

This is where you will see all of the news that those that you follow or have in circles have posted, and you can comment and share, and so on, from here.

Profile page

This is the place where you can see all of your own posts and share your content with those in your circles. From a search point of view, the more people who have you in their circles the better, because Google knows you are real and not spam, and also because if so many people are interested in what you have to say, it figures you are an authority.

People page

This is where you can find people to put in circles and see who has you in circles too.

Communities page

There is a whole array of communities you might want to join, so see what interests you and dive into a conversation. Communities are a great way to share and contribute to a common interest group and meet new people at the same time; they are great for online networking. From foodies to football, book clubs to inspiration, there is something for all by way of photo sharing, one to one (or more) in a Hangout or taking part in events and, just like Facebook, you can invite your Google+ buddies to the group.

Other functions

Google+ has other functions in common with some of the more popular platforms, namely hashtags and events.

Hashtags

When you post something on your page, hashtags will automatically be included for you, which is a great help if you're forgetful, like me! You can then change them and/or add more in.

Events

From your home page, you can create and share events just as you can on Facebook. You can add an image, choose whether to allow your friends to invite others or not, and decide exactly who you want to invite rather than just posting it publicly on your page. Fill in the rest of the event details such as time, date and location and you are all set to go.

Videos

As Google also owns YouTube, video integration is very easy. If you want to post a video, you have the option of either uploading it to your page, finding other people's videos on YouTube and linking to them or searching through your own video content list on YouTube. You can even record video from the video link.

Conclusion of chapter 12

Consider how Google+ can work for you. In short, if you are a bricks-and-mortar business, you need a Google+ page as people will be searching for you via Google to find your location and opening hours. If you're not a bricks-and-mortar business, then create your page and only update it with content occasionally, but put your efforts into a platform better suited to your business.

CHAPTER 13
Making your website work

Key areas we will cover in chapter 13:

✓ what SEO is and why you need it

✓ getting the most out of your website

✓ basic search engine optimisation (SEO) tips

✓ growing your site

✓ encouraging visitors.

One of the great things about social media is that it pushes traffic back to your website, where your visitors will find more information about your services or products. There are a few more things you can change very easily to improve your site's search-engine results and also impress your visitors. I had a chat with two professional SEO companies to make sure I had everything bang up to date for you, and the following is what Glenn Marvin (managing partner of SureFire Search Marketing) and Richard Conway from Pure SEO came up with.

What is SEO?

Search engine optimisation (SEO):

▶ is a marketing discipline focused on growing visibility in organic (non-paid) search engine results

▶ encompasses both the technical and creative elements required to improve rankings, drive traffic and increase awareness in search engines

▶ has many aspects, from the words on your page to the way other sites link to you on the web

▶ is sometimes simply a matter of making sure your site is structured in a way that search engines understand

▶ isn't just about building search-engine-friendly websites. It's about making your site better for people too.

Why does my website need SEO?

The majority of web traffic is driven by the major commercial search engines: Google, Bing and Yahoo!. Although social media and other types of traffic can generate visits to your website, search engines are the primary method of navigation for most Internet users. This is true whether your site provides content, services, products, information or just about anything else.

Search engines are unique in that they provide targeted traffic — that is, people looking for what you offer. They are the roadways that make this happen. If search engines cannot find your site or add your content to their databases, you miss out on incredible opportunities to drive traffic to your site.

Search queries (the words that users type into the search box) carry extraordinary value. Experience has shown that search-engine traffic can make (or break) an organisation's success.

Targeted traffic to a website can provide publicity, revenue and exposure like no other marketing channel. Investing in SEO can have an exceptional rate of return compared to other types of marketing and promotion.

Search engines are smart, but they still need help. The major engines are always working to improve their technology to trawl the web more deeply and return better results for users. However, there is a limit to how search engines can operate. Whereas the right SEO can net you thousands of visitors and increased attention, the wrong moves can hide or bury your site deep in the search results where visibility is minimal.

In addition to making content available to search engines, SEO also helps boost rankings so that content will be placed where searchers will more readily find it. The internet is becoming increasingly competitive, and those companies that perform SEO will have a decided advantage when it comes to visitors and customers.

Get the most out of your website

There are some quick and simple areas that you can focus on to make your website work better for you.

Page title tags

A title tag is the main text that describes an online document. Title elements have long been considered one of the most important on-page SEO elements (the most important being overall content), and appear in three key places: browsers, search engine results pages and external websites.

Google typically displays the first 50 to 60 characters of a title tag, or as many characters as will fit into a 512-pixel display.

If you keep your titles under 60 characters, you can expect at least 95 per cent of your titles to display properly.

A title tag should:

▶ contain the keywords that relate to that page

▶ be no more than 69 characters in length

▶ be relevant to the content on that page

▶ be unique for every page.

Page description tags (meta descriptions)

Page description tags or meta descriptions sit on each page, again buried at the top of the page for the robots, but humans can also see them when they do a search with Google and the descriptions of the website pages come up.

It's important that these are filled in as they are the descriptions that you and I see when we decide whether to click on that particular search result or the next one. These short paragraphs are your opportunity to advertise content to searchers and to let them know exactly whether the given page contains the information they're looking for.

Think of a meta description as your Google search result advertising copy. It draws readers to a website from the results page. Crafting a readable, compelling description using important keywords can get more people to click on the links to your site. Therefore, a call to action is a good idea. The description needs to be 156 characters or fewer, as this is all that will appear in the search result, and it should be relevant to the page it relates to. Every page on the website should have a unique description.

Ask yourself what makes you click on a particular link when you do a search. Search for your own business and see what your page descriptions say: do they make you want to click the link for more information or are your competitors' links more compelling?

To update your page title tags and meta descriptions you will need to have access into the 'back end' of your website where the coding sits: some content-management systems (such as WordPress) will allow you into these areas to add them in. If not, it's back to your web person.

Content

Have you ever been asked to provide content for your web developers to add to your website? This is by far the biggest challenge most business owners face when it comes to good-quality SEO in the modern digital age. Stepping back from the day-to-day grind of running a business and putting a creative hat on to write compelling, engaging, relevant information about each and every product and service you offer can be mind numbing. For many it just goes into the too hard basket and a last-minute hastily written page of information is thrown together as deadlines loom.

Over the past few years, Google has made a concerted effort to value the overall experience of its users. A result of this is that Google now places greater emphasis on the overall value of your content than on the specific keywords it contains.

As business owners we are often so caught up in what we know about our business that we make the mistake of using industry terminology and acronyms rather than laypersons' terms (for example, a doctor may use the term 'haematoma' rather than 'bruise'). Before you write your copy it certainly pays to research the common terms used when talking about *and* searching for your products and services. Talk to your non-industry friends, use the Google keyword planner—www.adwords.google.com/home/tools/keyword-planner—and get a good feel for the terminology you should use. The great thing about Google's approach to overall context and intent is you can mix the terminology up and you definitely do not need to repeat the same words over and over (our industry term for that is 'keyword stuffing').

Does this mean that you shouldn't optimise your content for keywords? No! The search engine still relies on keywords to some extent to understand the relevance of your content, but it has improved at understanding the context of the content. Keyword stuffing is dead and can hurt both your rankings and your website performance.

Basic rules of thumb for writing content

- Have a separate page for each product and service you offer.

- Write a minimum of 300 words per page, but aim for 1000 or more if you can.

- The first couple of paragraphs should focus on the core offering—feel free to use bullet points in this area.

- Talk about the benefits, not just the features, of the products or services you offer. People want to know how you are going to solve their problem, not just read technical jargon.

- Look at other high-performing websites in other competitive markets around the world to get ideas *but* avoid copying and pasting from other websites as Google recognises duplicated content.

- When you have written the content, take a breath, look at your competitors' websites and ask yourself if the content you have written deserves to be promoted above that of your competitors. Base this on the quality of the content you have written, *not* on the quality of your product or service compared to theirs.

Headlines

In website jargon, headlines are called H1 tags. The term 'H1 tags' simply refers to the main heading. When someone is searching for 'drains unblocked', the Google robots rush out and find all of the pages that have that search term on the page, they sort them into order and they give you the results. Whether that search term is in the page content or in the headline, how many times it appears and a bunch of other variables will determine where your website listing will come up. As no-one really knows how the Google algorithm runs, we can only work with the bits that we do know. With our previous example, 'drains unblocked' appears in the headline, while the rest of the content uses slightly different words such as 'drainage' and 'drain laying'. When the robots find the pages with the search terms required, they sort the pages into order of importance, working from the top of the page down. As H1 tags are at the top of the page, you have a better chance of being found if you have those search terms in your headings.

Title tags vs H1 tags: commonalities and differences

Both tags should provide titles that represent the overall message of your web page, so the best way to optimise title tags and H1 tags is to write for your readers while following SEO best practices.

The main differences are:

▶ Title tags appear in search engines and the web browser's title bar.

▶ H1 tags appear within the body text (ideally near the top of the web page).

▶ Search engines give more weight to title tags than H1 tags.

Some best practices for H1 page heading tags include:

▶ Have exactly one unique H1 tag per page.

▶ Ensure the H1 tag acts as a meaningful title for the page content.

▶ Use meaningful keywords in the H1 tag.

▶ If it makes sense, add a geographic term to the page heading.

To create an H1 tag for your web page content, use your focus keyword phrase word for word in your H1 tag. Keep the text succinct and to the point. There is no length requirement for the H1 tag, but it should make sense to the person visiting your page so they can quickly identify what the page is about.

Uploading PDFs

You can upload PDF files to get your page ranking higher. Search robots can now read PDF files that you add into your pages and as these are usually content-rich, they are great to use.

Some PDF ideas

Any PDFs you add to your website will not only add value for your website visitors but also be read by the robots. Examples of PDFs that you could add are:

- industry reports
- white papers
- articles you have had published elsewhere
- more information about your products or services.

Image alt tags

These are alternative tags used on images. Their primary function is to enable a visually impaired person, who may not be able to see the image, to understand what it is by using their audio website reader tools. Also, if an image fails to load properly, the alternative text that appears will again enable you to understand what the image is about. Additionally, if someone is searching just for images, your alternative description may well come up in their search.

When you set your alt tags up for each image on your website, you need to not only add a proper description but also include your keywords again. Going back to our blocked drains, a picture on the home page of Danny and his truck might have the alt tag 'Danny's Drainage unblocking drains'. You get the picture?

Activity 2

Make sure you have added the following to your website:

- headlines or H1 tags
- keywords in your content
- meta description keywords
- page description tags
- page titles
- alt tags.

Link building

Link building refers to how many links are pointing to your site from other sites, and is an important part of optimising your site. Having lots of links pointing to your site from other site sends the robots a message that your page must be important — otherwise why would others link to you? The issue here is that not all links are equal as the authority of the page that is linking to you has a lot to do with it.

Google looks at the quality of the links coming to your site, not just the quantity, as an indicator of trust and value. To put this into context, would you value five links to Danny's Drainage from random Russian blog sites?

Can you get an article published on your local or national newspaper's website or a TV station's site with a link back to yours?

A word of warning about companies that offer link exchanges through spam emails. They may sound like a good deal at the time as they link to you and you link to them. However, in reality what happens is you link to them and they return the link; then, a couple of weeks later they unlink from you, which just leaves your link to them in place—not very fair, but common practice. The only one to win that game is the initiator of the link swap. In practice, exchanging links has little to no value. The only reason to do it would be if the other website is very relevant to your business. For example, Danny's Drainage may have a link from and a link to a website that is an industry body.

One of the best ways of getting good-quality links pointing to your page is to create high-quality, engaging information—something we call 'link bait' in the industry. This is where you have something on your website that organically makes people want to link to you. Examples of link bait could be:

▶ a free ebook

▶ an infographic

▶ a high-quality industry blog.

Google search console (previously known as Webmaster Tools)

Go to www.google.com/webmasters/tools and take a look around because here you will find a whole bunch of website backend information that you don't get in your analytics, such as security and author statistics. It's free so you may as well use the information provided.

Extra URLs

Most companies have just one website with one website address, but have you thought about using several web addresses and pointing them all to the one website? If you are wondering why on earth you would want to do that, here's why:

▶ You may have a long company name.

▶ You may have a hard-to-pronounce company name.

▶ You may have a hard-to-spell or hard-to-hear company name.

▶ You wish to add keywords to your URL address.

▶ You don't want anyone else to buy that name.

Natural or clean URLs

When creating new pages throughout your website, give some thought to how the URL of the page will look, and by that I mean is it simple enough? When you are directing someone to a particular page from, say, a TV commercial or newspaper advertisement, you want to give them something that is easily remembered and easily heard. For example, the 'Spark's Tech in a Sec' ad on TV always points back to its web page: www.spark.co.nz/help/techinasec/ rather than something like www.spark.co.nz/124567techpage or something else equally hard to remember.

Keep the URL simple and logical and make sure it contains keywords where possible. The speaking page on my site is called 'Social media speaker', which is exactly what the page is all about, and the page name is easily remembered and easy to pass on.

Grow your site

Each and every time you add new content to your website, the robots take note. Think of the robots as mice and your website content as their food, and boy do they like to eat. Each time you develop a new page on your site, they run off, devour it and head back home. Once they have done this a couple of times in a month they begin to see that you are providing for them on a regular basis and they make a mental note to call back to your site more frequently than to other sites that have not provided for them in a while. Keeping your website pages very active will stand you in good stead with Google and the search rankings, as this is one area they monitor. Sites that don't get this attention — and there are many — are limiting their chances of being found. If you look at the main news sites, new and fresh content is added at least daily, so they grow massively over the course of a year.

Most websites are built within some sort of template, which means adding a new page is simply a matter of clicking a button or two and — hey presto! — you need only to add keyword-rich, interesting content for your readers.

Having a widget showing your latest social media posts is a great idea as content changes regularly when you make new posts.

Google AdWords

This is a great way to get visitors to your site, but I am not going to go into that in this book as it is a bit of a minefield and I suggest you get a professional to set it up for you. You can, however, set it up yourself if you are prepared to put a bit of effort into monitoring and tweaking your ads when needed. Set yourself a monthly budget that you can afford and give it a go. I would recommend getting in touch with someone who really knows it inside out and take their advice.

Claim your 'Google My Business' page

Ever wondered how sometimes when you search, there is a map that shows up and a bunch of listings, all with the little red Google location pin on them, usually from A to Z? That is where Google My Business comes in.

Go to www.google.com/business/ and set yours up. For it to work properly, you need to make sure it is fully filled out and kept up to date.

When it comes to adding your address, you will need to provide an actual physical address and Google will send you a postcard with a verification code on it to activate your listing. When you have filled it all out, work on getting some client reviews on your page. Google uses reviews as another bookmark. You may have noticed you can link your business page to a Google+ page here too.

Activity 3

Claim your 'Google My Business' page for extra exposure.

Conclusion of chapter 13

Your website says a lot about your brand so do make sure people can understand it and navigate it easily and that the robots can find it when someone is searching for whatever it is you have to offer. By following the easy steps in this chapter, you will be giving your website a fighting chance to generate results for you.

CHAPTER 14

Staying safe

Key areas we will cover in chapter 14:

✓ staying safe as an individual

✓ security for your business

✓ geotagging.

Once you have opened various social media accounts for your business, use them. If you let them go to waste and nobody takes responsibility for them, you may not be aware if they ever get breached with malicious posts and messages going out on your behalf. The notes that follow are not meant to scare you, but to arm you with knowledge so you and your business can stay safe online.

Security for your business accounts

We all make mistakes, and human error is something we need to be aware of. A staff member posts to the wrong account (it has happened — it should have been their personal account) and suddenly something is on your company page you'd rather the world didn't see — and it was completely accidental. By using a platform such as Hootsuite, you can monitor the posts being sent out — including who sent them — before they go, giving you peace of mind that posts won't accidentally go wrong.

Malicious posts — perhaps from a disgruntled employee — are another thing to consider. A bad day at the office can be catastrophic if employees are able to rant and rave publicly, as some team members did at HMV when they were being made redundant.

It's wise to implement a social media policy regarding what can and can't be posted. Usually, a simple sentence such as 'not bringing the company name into disrepute when using digital channels' inserted into the employment contract is enough. Add relevant training to the team keeping them up to date and you won't go far wrong. Don't assume that just because they tweet a lot or have a Facebook profile page they know how to market and communicate online effectively and represent your company. The digital space is changing constantly and the team needs to keep up with tools and trends for your success. Also, allocate a digital champion: the person who will oversee the whole strategy to make sure it's implemented correctly.

Don't let issues such as these stop you operating online; just make sure you have steps in place to stop incidents happening. You wouldn't stop your team from communicating on the telephone fearing they may say the wrong thing, so don't with the online channels — give them the knowledge to do it right instead.

When it comes to your own personal profile pages, remember you are in control of your own privacy settings, *and* what you post is entirely up to you. If you don't want to add your date of birth, then don't. Be comfortable with what you share and don't be swayed into thinking you have to post the same type of posts as some of your friends.

Geotagging yourself

Geotagging is the attaching of GPS coordinates, or geographical metadata, to posts, videos and images that are then uploaded to the internet. It tells anyone who is interested from where that post or picture was uploaded, essentially allowing the platform to map your uploads. It's common practice for most, if not all, social media sites to do this — they've been doing it for quite some time so it's nothing new.

We have been slowly conditioned by Facebook, Instagram, Apple and others to give out our current location by way of geotagging as a way of showing people exactly where we are. It's also valuable marketing data, so businesses can send messages through apps and sites to prospective customers nearby and entice them to use their product or service.

Let's look at what that means for you as an individual.

Here's an example. You check into your favourite café mid morning using Facebook's check-in prompt. The GPS coordinates are now in place and anyone who can see your post will know exactly where you are. The post itself shows on your timeline, telling your friends where you are — but what you can't easily see is the coordinates. However, they are there to be found. If you have a regular coffee meeting every Friday morning at the same time at the same place, a stalker or investigator could easily find out your whereabouts. It also signifies where you are not — at home or work perhaps.

Another common post that appears in newsfeeds is people at airports checking in on Facebook, usually with their boarding pass in the photo, which reveals their name, flight and seat number. Not only is the information clearly visible to read, if you happened to have a barcode scanner, you'd probably be privy to their frequent flyer number too, something usually kept very private for obvious reasons. The intention of this is usually to show off where their next adventure is, but they are essentially giving out private information about themselves that could make them a potential target. If that's something you do yourself, maybe it's best that you don't advertise where you're going and for how long, particularly if your security settings are set wide open for anyone to see into.

The Kim Kardashian robbery received a lot of media attention, both good and bad. Was a geotag to blame? Who knows, but if you tweet a picture of your wonderful diamond necklace or your very rare Fabergé egg, *then any thief worth their salt could easily find it*. Yet we still use these platforms and share our locations without any concern or consideration for the consequences that are attached. For example, while on safari, tourists will happily post pictures of valuable animals in their natural habitat, all the while pointing the exact location out to potential poachers.

Geotagging your business

If you run a day spa on a busy road in your town, knowing who is nearby would be really helpful. For example, you might have spare appointments one day or just want to market to people who haven't been customers before and don't know about your business. By using Facebook's ads targeted to those close to your bricks-and-mortar business, you are able to get your message in front of their eyeballs. If they just happen to be surfing their newsfeed as they walk home past your business, Facebook will place your ad right under their nose. It will even tell you how many people in your target market are in the area who you could show the ad to, which is useful information for your business for future advertising too.

Your history is recorded as you move about from place to place — you don't even need to be obvious and check in for that information to be generated. I have an iPhone, like many people, that tracks my whereabouts automatically because the default setting is 'On'. If someone had access to my phone, they could easily see all the places I've visited including the times I have been at home, making any movement patterns obvious. I shared this snippet of information with a client over coffee once and she looked back at her own history on her phone wondering just where it was she went every Sunday morning. Church! Anyone who had access to her phone would know exactly when would be the best time to pop into her home uninvited, knowing exactly where she would be — and for how long.

However, of course, you can turn this setting off. On most phones you go to 'settings', 'privacy', 'location services' (ironic, really, that it's under 'privacy') and turn it 'off'. Or, if you prefer, you can turn off location services (GPS) for your phone's camera. If you have an iPhone, scroll down to 'system services', 'frequent locations' and take a look at where you've been and how many times! You can also turn 'frequent locations' off and clear your history. However, if you still want to use 'maps', you will need 'location services' turned on, so just turn it off on your photos if you prefer.

Your location history reveals your buying habits, your interests, where you hang out, where you work and when you check others in who are with you or they do the reverse to you — even who you hang out with.

The story that follows is one company's experience after it got a one-star review on its Facebook page and how it handled it. While it's not particularly about staying safe, it is about the negative side of being active online and handling a negative review well.

Real story: Life Care Consultants

I can't recall when I first heard, 'You need to have a social media presence', but I assume it was at least eight years ago. I can still recall the, 'Oh yeah, you are probably right, but what does it look like and how do I do it?' thought.

I am, and have been for the past 23 years, in business — a huge advocate for face-to-face relationship building to build sales and ongoing revenue — so social media was always something I knew we should be involved with, but my focus was to build a

(continued)

Real story: Life Care Consultants *(cont'd)*

motivated and enthusiastic sales team. This sales team needed to love meeting people, be fantastic at building relationships and be talented at closing a deal.

I hear all of you who have engaged with this same goal saying how difficult it is. Though it sounds simple, it is an extremely difficult task. Great salespeople are hard to find!

What I didn't realise until Life Care Consultants started to work with social media, was how it can help the sales and can do 'some of the leg work'. We have always used call cycles to ensure we keep in touch with our clients. The frequency of these is dependent on how much a client spends with us. However, we may not communicate for up to a year with clients who spend a little but have been our clients for, say, the past 20 years. Yet, during this time, things may have changed without us knowing. Enter social media!

The advantage, as well as the disadvantage of social media, is the public space and the reach. Even the president of the United States has chosen Twitter over mainstream media.

We have just had our best year ever and coincidentally it was about a year ago when we started working on building our brand online and establishing our social media presence. We have made other changes within the year as well so the social media presence can't take the full credit. However, it has certainly helped in a number of ways, including listening and acting on things quickly.

In some industries—in particular the hospitality industry—businesses live and die by their reviews, and the pendulum has certainly swung in favour of the consumer. A nasty or critical review can have a devastating effect and, like any negative feedback, it is often not the feedback that's the problem; it is more about putting it right. I don't believe any business gets things 100 per cent right 100 per cent of the time, so we need to be timely, appropriate and professional in fixing things when we 'muck up', even if it is only in the eyes of the consumer.

The public space and the reach are great when everything is positive, consumers are happy and businesses can have their presence felt. However, when there is a disgruntled consumer, things can turn challenging very quickly.

Life Care Consultants is a training establishment so we do receive reviews, but not to the same extent as other industries that are reviewed on Trip Advisor and similar sites. We get a lot of great feedback, mainly via email, sometimes by phone and often during meetings with our clients.

When I got a call from one of our account managers one morning at 7.15, my thoughts were, 'What could have gone wrong?' He was devastated that an individual from one of our major clients had published a really nasty review on our company Facebook page and given us a 'one-star' rating. The reviewer was also really derogatory about his employer choosing us. We looked at his Facebook profile, which was easy because his privacy settings were set to 'everyone' and saw he had posted a similar review there too. A number of his 'friends' commented, gave him sympathy and built on his negativity. When we looked at his other posts we could see he was one of those characters who complain and grizzle about everything. However, this didn't really help us—although it made us feel a little better!

I replied to his post on his personal profile page with a comment and my phone number, acknowledging his disappointment with our service and with an invitation to ring me to discuss his concerns. Our account manager rang the client to ensure the feedback was isolated and not the general consensus (we normally get really good feedback from this client).

We also replied to his nasty comments on our Facebook page, offering to discuss what happened between his positive feedback

(continued)

Real story: Life Care Consultants *(cont'd)*

on the day of the training and this review three weeks later. He then came back to us with abuse about contacting his employer! At this point we really needed to put a stop to this so I posted one last message saying my job is to ensure our clients are happy and hence I needed to ensure his opinion was a one-off and once again invited him to contact me directly to discuss his concerns. We never heard from him again, and I'd like to think the damage was minimal—but you never know.

This whole scenario identified the risks involved in the public arena that social media sits in. However, the risks also come with advantages, which include the fact that going back a number of years we would never have been able to reach such a large audience for such a small investment.

Like everything in life we can't keep 100 per cent of people happy 100 per cent of the time—and unhappy people now have a public forum where they can voice their 'unhappiness'. It is the putting it right that matters, and the benefits of being proactive online far outweigh the drawbacks when it is done properly and professionally. We wouldn't be without our online presence now and I wish we'd got moving with it a lot sooner.

Conclusion of chapter 14

Be aware of security for yourself and your business and take steps to mitigate any errors. Take a look at your privacy settings on your smartphone and choose what locations you want to share with others. Take control yourself.

CHAPTER 15
Promoting yourself and getting results

Key areas we will cover in chapter 15:

✓ encouraging visitors to your sites

✓ ensuring consistency between your online and offline brands.

Promote your social media efforts

Let's look at how to get that all-important exposure for your social media sites so that other people know you exist and can engage and communicate with you, all of which leads to sales.

Email signature

If you are using the professional version of Outlook you can add the icon images of your chosen sites to your email signature and hyperlink them to the relevant pages — so you can have one linking to your Facebook page, one to your Twitter page, one to your LinkedIn profile or company page, and so on. If you don't want to use the icon images, you can simply hyperlink a short piece of text such as 'follow us on Facebook' and it will do the same job but you are including a call to action at the same time.

Your emails go to people everywhere, not just to people in your place of work. So this is a really easy way to get some exposure for your sites, particularly when you are sending an email to a prospect as it gives that recipient a chance to see a whole lot more about your company. Your friends and family who you email will also get the benefit of keeping up with your business side if they wish, even down to the real estate agent you recently emailed about a possible move, or the travel agent about a holiday you have just confirmed.

For those who use an email program such as Gmail, there is an option for you too called www.wisestamp.com. It enables you to build your email signature and then include links to sites such as LinkedIn, Twitter and many more. You can even add random quotes that change on every email, or your username for Skype, and filter in your latest tweets. You never know where your email will end up, and I know I have definitely got business from my email signature.

Business cards

Some companies still include their fax number on their cards and I guess that in some industries a fax machine may still be used, but if you think about yours, how often does it ring with anything that's not spam? That's if you even have one.

Use this valuable space to promote your page addresses and usernames for Skype and Twitter so that others can choose which way to communicate with you and also find further information about your company easily. Use both sides of your card so that it doesn't look too cramped. If you have to use a corporate business card that does not have all of this information on it, think about getting a second card printed with your alternative details that you can pass out alongside your corporate one.

As an aside, while we are talking about what your business card could have on it, does it have what you actually do on it too? I don't mean 'Director' or another title, but if a 14-year-old picked up your card, would they understand what it is you do when they read it?

My card says 'Linda Coles, Author, Speaker and Trainer. Building relationships online', so anyone who picks up my card can see instantly what I do. What does yours say?

Printed media

People can contact you in so many different ways so wherever you would put your telephone number, think about putting your social media page details there too. Print media is certainly no different, so think about these ideas and see if any could apply to you:

▶ menus

▶ appointment cards

▶ flyers

▶ posters

▶ postcards

▶ greeting cards

▶ folders

▶ calendars

▶ stickers

▶ vouchers

▶ bookmarks

▶ corporate gifts.

Don't forget to add your social site details to any ads you run in the press and telephone directories. In fact, think about all of the areas you publish your telephone number or web address and add them in.

> ## Activity 1
>
> Where will you promote your efforts? Make a list of the areas you can utilise.

Vehicle signage

Hold on, I don't mean you have to go and get your whole car sign-written at huge expense, but why not do at least the back window of your car or service vehicles? I paid a few dollars for my web address to be put in my back window and I know people have seen it because they have commented on it.

I was once at a set of traffic lights in town when I looked across to the car beside me. I thought the driver looked familiar but the lights changed and off I went. When I got back to the office, there was a LinkedIn message for me from the person in that car! He had seen my back window, realised it was me and was simply saying hello. I have never actually met that person yet, only chatted on LinkedIn, but maybe one day...I have also had people toot their horn and wave to me and I've absolutely no idea who they are but they may have chatted to me online somewhere (either that, or they are nutters).

TV and radio

If you are lucky enough to be able to afford TV or radio advertising, the same applies here. Many magazine and current affairs TV shows advertise their Facebook name at the end of each episode, inviting you over to the page after the program to leave your views and comments about the show's topics.

For big brands that are running promotions and giveaways on TV, it's the ideal place to send your traffic. You no longer need to spend large amounts of money on separate websites and applications for big promotions. Just make use of Facebook.

Using your Facebook page address rather than your website means you only need a short and easy-to-remember URL. This is because the web address of any Facebook page will always be www.facebook.com followed by a forward slash and the page name: www.facebook.com/yourpagename. That means you then only need to tell people to go to your Facebook page 'yourpagename' and that's all they have to remember. Bear this in mind when you set up your URL in the beginning as once you have named your page it is virtually impossible to change it.

Website

Your website is also an obvious place to post links back to your social sites as your web address is usually posted on all of your printed media. Many websites simply place the icon images for Facebook, Twitter, and so on, on their front page somewhere at the bottom and hope that will suffice, but it could be done better. As visitors to any site, we now expect to see them top right of the page, so follow suit.

If your web designer is able to incorporate the icon images into the site's template so they appear automatically on every page, that would be ideal, but if not, consider adding the images to the home page, 'About' page and contact page at the very least.

Social box plug-in

These plug-ins, or widgets, allow your website visitors to read the last content you loaded onto your Facebook page, Twitter feed or Pinterest—or whichever plug-in you are using—and become a fan or follower of your page without ever leaving your website.

Your visitors can also see who else is a fan, and if any of their friends are, if it's the Facebook plug-in. Google will help you find the plug-ins for you and the HTML code to install in your website as it has instructions on how to create the plug-in you require. The code will need to be installed by your web person if you can't get into the coding area yourself. You may want to add it to your blog site also, if you have one.

Page backgrounds

Your Twitter page, LinkedIn profile page and YouTube page will allow you to create and install an image for the whole of the background, so this is another place to add your other social site details. I use a copy of the same image from my Facebook page for continuity because it already has my logo, my picture and my contact details, so it really is a no-brainer.

Voicemail

This may seem a crazy idea, but why not? 'I'm sorry I'm not able to take your call at the moment, but why not visit my Facebook page in the meantime...'. Think of the exposure.

Newsletter

If you are regularly sending out newsletters to your database, your social media links need to be on there too. I use a call-to-action text link within my newsletter as well as image icons at the end to promote the sites. For example, your message may say, 'We have had some very interesting comments on our Facebook wall about the new chocolate-flavoured spread...'. Hyperlink the 'Facebook wall' text to go through directly to your page where they can read more. 'Write your wish list on our Facebook wall' is a good call to action and very easy for your readers to do and have a bit of fun with.

Activity 2

Make sure you have your social media addresses or links in these areas:

- email signature
- business cards
- website
- blog
- Facebook page
- Twitter page
- LinkedIn page
- other social sites
- all print material
- newsletter text.

Is your online message the same as your offline message?

You may recall in chapter 1, I mention a company director whose prospect had contacted him after doing his due diligence and found some discrepancies between the company's offline and online messages—it was not practising what it preached. Is your message consistent across all your forms of marketing?

Double-check the following:

▶ Is your strap line or brand promise on all of your printed and online marketing?

▶ Is your brand consistent on all of your email signatures?

- ▶ Do your LinkedIn profiles follow your corporate look but with some personal individuality?

- ▶ Are you proud of all of your tweets or do they need reining in?

- ▶ Does your website mirror everything in your marketing arsenal?

And if your message is consistent, is your style sheet consistent across your brand? By that I mean do you have a few branding rules in place so that visually you look consistent wherever someone may be looking at you? For example, what is the colour code of your logo, and does it match your business cards?

Rules simply give us a framework within which to work so that the edges don't get blurred on what is acceptable and what isn't, so it makes sense to set up a style sheet to keep it easy.

Use fonts consistently

What font do you use when you are typing a quotation or letter and is it the same font as you use in your email? Does it also match the font on your website, and what about your brochures and business cards? If you use Arial 11 in all of your articles, but Calibri 12 on your website, that is not consistent and one of them may need to change.

Think about which font and which size you should have for the following on your online sites:

- ▶ headlines
- ▶ subheadings
- ▶ paragraphs.

I have included a checklist to help you make sure everything is covered.

Checklist

Design checklist for continuity:

- website font
- website headlines
- website subheadings
- website paragraphs
- email signature colour
- email signature text and logo
- Twitter page background
- Facebook page images
- YouTube channel background
- LinkedIn profile background image
- your other social sites
- email newsletter font
- email newsletter images
- blog font
- blog images
- all sites linked to each other where possible.

So now you've created an audience or community, your social efforts are thriving, your content plan is working and your website is getting even more traffic than before. Everything you've been doing up until now has all been pointing to getting more sales. Yes, you want to be cool and friendly online, but ultimately it's sales you're after.

Your website

We covered it off, but here is something you need to think about. When someone finds you, wants what you have on offer and hits the 'contact' button, it's got to be easy and seamless with an immediate response. Forget boxes to be filled in; give them an email link or telephone that is manned and jump straight on it. Studies have shown the hottest time to get back to an email enquiry is within the first five minutes. Yes, only five. Forget pretending you're super busy; reply to their enquiry immediately, even if it's just to say you'll follow back up with them later in the day. But get in contact before they go to your competition.

Direct messages

These are no different from getting an email enquiry and should be responded to quickly. Obviously, if someone has contacted you via Facebook after hours, they are not expecting a reply there and then, but do check for messages within the relevant platform daily. While many will notify you via email that a message is waiting, from my experience it can be a bit hit and miss.

I asked a recruitment company how they approach social media. This is their story.

Real story: RWR Group

We are a multinational specialist recruitment agency with 16 offices across three markets. Our specialist industry sectors include retail and hospitality and the brands Retailworld and Hospoworld are market leaders in their fields. The brands' success and identity have developed via disciplined marketing led activity that has enabled industry engagement and alignment.

As our social media strategy has progressed, the inclusion of social campaigns into our marketing mix was inevitable. Getting our message right for the targeted audiences and measuring the impact was important for us to know that this part of our marketing strategy was effective.

We didn't get it right the first time!

After a reasonable investment with an outsourced specialist content provider/social media agency went horribly wrong we sought further advice and a strategic reset.

Just like our brands have targeted niche audiences, so too do each of the social media platforms and getting cut through comes down to clear goals, aligned content and not compromising volume for quality.

We clearly defined our target markets across the various platforms and the voice that each of our content pieces needed to have to align with our brand message and reputation.

Here are some considerations that we recommend you think about when you look at your content marketing/social media:

- *You have a short window to grab someone's attention.*
  Keep your message short—get to your point quickly.

(continued)

Real story: RWR Group *(cont'd)*

- *Images work.* Generate interest in your brand; bring the traffic to your website to provide more information and build a stronger relationship in your environment.

- *Measure your results.* We noticed increased referral traffic via Google Analytics.

- *Mix it up.* Have a variety of content.

- *Use content marketing to position your voice of expertise.* Stick to your specialty.

- *Be careful using outsourced content writers.* The best content is authentic and factual—not written to feature high in SEO. It can be good for the SEO robots, but can lead to a poor audience experience and high bounce rates off your site.

- *Don't get stars in your eyes.* Over-investment of time and money is very easy to achieve—understand how content and social fit into your overall marketing strategy and goals.

Ask yourself, 'What outcomes do I want?' Are they:

- brand recognition

- redirected web traffic from social to your own site/shop

- interaction within the platform

- conversion/sales?

Take yourself on a social journey and get educated on the potential and reach that a well-executed content and social strategy can have. Content marketing and social media remain important features of our overall marketing and brand strategy and are now just part of what we do.

Conclusion of chapter 15

Long gone are the days of just a single website representing your brand online. There are now many more places to find and be found. As long as everything you do has professional consistency across it, you'll not go far wrong. Keep to your branding guidelines, colour schemes, fonts and tone and refresh header images regularly across the board for an up-to-date look. And get back to enquiries as they happen!

Wrap

I hope I have given you some ideas on how your business can make use of these online sites to seek and engage new prospects, and to add value for your current clients so that they stick around with you a good while longer. But it's all very well reading a book. You now have to put into practice what you have learned. Execute that plan!

Remember, you can always contact me through the website if you have any burning questions you need answered. I will be only too happy to help.

Until the next book, I raise my cup of tea to your online success!

Linda Coles

Appendix: Daisy's social media plan

Daisy's is a local flower shop with a great reputation and a loyal customer base. The team is thinking of expanding by opening another store in a neighbouring town. They would also like their online sales to increase nationally.

The team starts by putting together a social media plan (see table A1), where they brainstorm about the purpose, projected achievements and outcome of the social media campaign, and identify their short- and long-term social media objectives. After completing this they put together a SWOT analysis to identify their strengths and weaknesses, and to find out where the opportunities and threats will come from (see table A2). Finally, they complete the content plan (see table A3), which gives them an idea of what their social media campaign will be focusing on. In this case, they will be using Facebook to create dialogue with their customers (mainly women aged 35 to 50) in the hope that they become cheerleaders for the brand.

Table A1: Daisy's social media plan

What is the purpose?	What are our 12-month social media objectives?
• educate our customers on flowers and grow our brand name online • create a dialogue to engage with our customers	• 1000 likes and 1000 followers and continued customer reviews • understand what our customers want and value • be the number one choice for flowers online in the local area • page 1 of Google for local flowers
What will it achieve?	**What are our six-month social media objectives?**
• customers will get more from their bouquets • relationship building with us	• create 500 likes and 500 followers • understand our customers' desires
What is the outcome?	**What are our three-month social media objectives?**
• be seen as the expert in the flower field • understand our customers more	• create 200 likes, 200 followers, customer feedback on our wall • create dialogue with our customers to find out their desires
Our target market is:	**Measured by?**
female, 35–50, loves a little luxury	Google Analytics, followers, likes, shares, engagement, 5-star reviews
Owner:	**Team:**
Stella is accountable	All team members are free to submit articles and stories for inclusion, but Stella is accountable

Table A2: Daisy's SWOT analysis

Strengths	Weaknesses
• strong brand name in the local area • good online presence locally • great knowledgeable team • drive and enthusiasm • creativity • great delivery team with local knowledge	• only one location • not well known outside our location
Opportunities	**Threats**
• broaden our brand to a larger geographical area • be seen as the experts in our field • open more stores • educate our customers to get the most from their purchase • generate repeat business • focus on 'treat yourself everyday' displays for more repeat business	• other online and local florists • team could be poached by the competition • diminishing margin with cheaper competitors

Table A3: Daisy's content plan

What is your target market's BIGGEST problem, need or desire?	Themes for the quarter
• flowers in a hurry • a bouquet that shows their feelings • they have forgotten an event and need to make it up to that person • a great-looking bouquet • delivery when they need it	• Valentine's Day • Easter • love • continued flower care • quick care tips
Articles to write	**Useful videos**

• looking after your bouquet
 	
• origins of Valentine's Day
 	
• which flowers are in season during January, February and March
 	
• this year's fashionable colours
 	
• quick tips on creating your own small bouquet
 	
• what the flowers you choose mean
 	
• which flowers to buy the man in your life
	• Search YouTube for:
	
	  – Valentine's Day funny videos
	
	  – caring for your flowers.
	
	• Create a one-minute video on what we will be doing this Valentine's Day.
	
	• Create a one-minute video on alternative gifts for Easter this year.

Off-message questions	**Useful websites**
• What is the funniest Valentine's Day gift you have ever received? • Have you ever sent flowers too late? • Do you send Easter eggs to your loved ones? • How will you be celebrating Valentine's Day? • How will you be celebrating Easter?	• www.interflora.com.au • www.theflowercompany.com.au • www.valentines.com

Index